FREEDOM

I personally know all of these authors. I have done business with every one of them. It is amazing to work with people who have the same core values as you do. Every one of these people has the highest integrity, believe in each other, work hard and are Go Givers ... The road to financial freedom is awesome!!

~ Tom Olson

Over the years I've been involved with Dr. David Phelps and his group. I've enjoyed watching many of the doctors achieve a level of financial freedom they could hardly have imagined. How did they do it? Simply by leveraging the knowledge, connections and deal flow already inside this group.

Best of all, I've seen the doctors gain peace of mind as they rely less and less on the income from their practices. Any working professional will be inspired by the personal stories told by the doctors themselves in this book.

My hat's off to Dr. Phelps and everyone in his group who has taken action to achieve their dreams of financial freedom!

~ Dave Van Horn
President of PPR Note Co.

This is not just a splendid book; it is a spectacular one.... It can only be described as a labor of love for each of the authors, a fastidiously expressed and profusely illustrated account of their individual walks from education to practice to perceived achievement to actual financial freedom. Read this book or be prepared to never find your true purpose beyond a fat bank account.

~ Mark Jackson
Founder, InvestorCompsOnline
Expert Real Estate Valuation Training and Data
www.InvestorCompsOnline.com
Appraiser Secrets
Follow me on Twitter

FREEDOM

*Travel along with 15 doctors
who created enough passive income
to gain freedom*

DR. FORREST BRYANT

ISBN 13: 978-0-692089715-7
10: 0-692-89715-1

HIGH SPEED
P U B L I S H I N G

FOREWORD

Dr. Mike Abernathy

I have been known to say, bluntly, that being a solo practitioner dentist past age 50 can be a 99% fatal condition. This book is about the 1%, the ones who found their way off the treadmill. I am familiar with most of the authors and their stories. They probably won't ever make any money from this book, especially compared with their other financial successes inside and outside their practices, but in their stories you will quickly see their mission—to help others who are in the same place as they were not very long ago

INTRODUCTION

Almost daily we hear the sad news of how the average American is doing little or nothing to prepare themselves for the inevitable day when they will stop exchanging the hours of their lives for income, what I call transactional income. Many are convinced that the "retirement plan" that their place of employment has offered them, or social security or whatever, will take care of their needs. A few sad statistics show otherwise:

1. The average American family savings account balance is $4,220.
2. Adults under thirty-five have a negative savings rate of two percent.
3. The average American spends an astonishing 4.3 hours per day watching TV, but virtually no time planning the last thirty years of his/her life.
4. Fifty-nine percent of Americans say that running out of money in retirement is their number one fear, and yet they are not taking action to prevent that—likely because they do not know how!
5. Ninety-six percent of members of the American Dental Association retire to an income level below what they lived on while practicing! These are some of the highest wage earners in the country—proving that high income alone will not save you!
6. These shocking statistics do not even include the unfunded liabilities that are piling up by federal, state and local governments. In the future, the average American—you and your children—will be

responsible for inevitably higher taxes.

Ladies and gentlemen, if this is average, you cannot afford to be average! The fact that you have read past the first introductory sentences already tells me that you are not average, and yet, like so many United States citizens, you are confused by the bombardment of advertising from the "experts" on how to solve your individual problem. There is a mismatch between what is being sold to us by those that stand to benefit from their financial plans and what the evidence shows us would be most effective.

Sadly, we were ourselves guilty of being less than ideal in planning our financial freedom (that point at which you no longer need to trade your time for dollars) so if we sound a bit condescending in our assessment of those around us, the mirror could easily have been turned on us until just recently. I had convinced myself that I loved working so much that retirement from dentistry was not in my future, when the truth was my need to keep working was more about a fear that the only book we were going to write would be titled *Sixty-Four Ways to Cook with Alpo.*

Instead, we find ourselves co-writing a book on achieving financial freedom with an amazing group of people who are on the path with us. Not only with us, but helping us to move along the path faster. You will get to meet each of them in this book. All of these co-authors have put their names out there for you, and it is likely that one of them lives within a two-hour drive of you, and of course, all of them (including us) are just a phone call or email away. We have found answers that we simply must share with others. It is far too powerful to keep to ourselves.

The solution to your financial situation, and that of so many of our fellow citizens, is not going to come from the latest product or service offered by the financial industry. It is not going to come from that catchy TV ad that someone had about "your number." The solution is not going to come from our government. (Are you really surprised on that one?) It has to come from each of us taking charge of our own financial health. Nobody cares about your finances—truly cares—except you! If you do not take away anything from this book other than that, it has been worth the time to read it. We learned that lesson later than we should have, but fortunately, not too late.

For those of you who are ready to take charge of your financial future, this book is for you. For those of you who are frustrated with earning next to nothing or losing money on your investments, this book is for you. For those of you who do not see the path to reach your retirement goals, this book is for you. For those of you who are concerned about the economic future of your children, this book is for you. For those of you who are concerned about the economic future of our country, this book is for you, as well.

That is why the information presented here by my co-authors is so important. It is what we need to hear—practical, real world information taught with the wisdom of actual experiences and compassion. It is not "magic." It is not "get rich overnight." It is not "turn your money over to your financial wizard." The information here contains stories from real people who have found a way out of the average American trap. They have jumped in to write this book because just like you, they were searching for a better way. And now they are on the path to financial freedom, and they want to share it. They have learned the lesson that YOUR NETWORK IS YOUR NET WORTH. Accept my congratulations for reading this book and deciding to take control of your financial future. Study it well. Contact one of the authors, including us. You will feel more in control of your future than ever. This book has a powerful message. It may very well change the future for you and your family.

TABLE OF CONTENTS

Forrest Bryant

Dr. B's INVESTMENT LESSONS FOR ANY INVESTOR

I'm no guru, but I do have a pretty interesting story to tell. I spent twenty years as a dentist, starting out as an employee in someone else's practice, then becoming a co-owner, and eventually, the sole owner. I grew the practice over 500% in fifteen years, adding multiple locations with multiple doctors and hygienists.

In 2011, when serious health issues put an end to my days in the operatory, I stepped out of the clinical world and devoted my time to the business side of the practice. I continued to build the business over the next five years. When multiple companies began making inquiries about buying the business, I sold the entire operation in 2016.

I was approached by a large investment and insurance company to work for them as a financial advisor and planner. I knew my future was going to be about helping other business owners reach their goals, and I knew the knowledge I would attain working for the company would be critical. So for two years, I worked as a financial advisor helping high net worth families invest and grow their wealth, as well as protect that wealth and unearned wealth against catastrophe.

The insider knowledge I gained about investing in Wall Street and the stock market, along with intensive knowledge of personal and business insurance products, gave me a solid base to work from.

Naturally, as a financial planner, having the inside track was enlightening, but I felt conflicted and disappointed with the limited options available to my clients. I've been a real estate investor for the past twenty years. Initially, I fell into the same trap many doctors, dentists, and other high-income individuals fall into. I was looking for the big hits— the big speculative deals with the big payoffs. It's called *The Greater Fool Theory*, i.e. buying something and hoping someone else (a greater fool) comes along to pay you more than you paid for it. The problem with this theory is that you ride the wave of good fortune when there is an abundance of greater fools and get washed away with the tide when the greatest fool is you. Sometimes it works, and sometimes it doesn't.

Several years ago, I met Dr. David Phelps with *Freedom Founders*, and I shifted my thinking about real estate investing. I abandoned *The Greater Fool* method and started following Dr. Phelps' advice, which has made investing in real estate much safer by focusing on CASH FLOW investments like single-family homes in boring markets in middle America. There are lots of twists in Cash Flow investments such as private lending, private real estate funds, multi-family, and commercial projects.

It's not super sexy as investments go, but the returns are based on cash flow, not speculation. And that's the big difference in how some investors think. We don't care what the stock market does. If it goes up, then the real estate markets appreciate. And if the stock market crashes, like it did in 2007-2008, our rents will increase, and we will make more money either way. We don't ride the emotional stock market rollercoaster with its sudden highs and lows, and that makes life so much more enjoyable and keeps our money safe.

When I sat down to evaluate the returns of my stock market portfolio versus the returns of my real estate holdings, it was clear that real estate outperformed stocks with much less risk.

It became increasingly difficult for me to advise my financial clients to invest 100% of their money in the stock market (even though that's how financial planners and their companies get paid, i.e. commissions) when that wasn't what I felt was best for my own money. My integrity simply would not allow me to go there. There is a balance for investors who are open to learning about alternative investments.

Thus began the soul searching that became my newest venture, *High Speed Alliance.* My goals were to give doctors and CEOs another way to invest their money by showing them alternatives to Wall Street for a portion or even all of their portfolios, and other ways to make tax-free and tax-deferred investments that mainstream financial advisors would never tell them about. So, I have come up with a set of guide-lines (or lessons) on investing. They are as follows:

LESSON NUMBER 1: Risk and Speculative Investments

Rarely does a get-rich-quick scheme work. I learned this lesson the hard way. I graduated dental school in 1997 and started investing in high-tech stocks that had a meteoric rise. They earned incredible re-turns for several years, then the tech bubble of 1999–2000 burst, and most tech stocks (including mine) came crashing back down to earth.

It wasn't a huge amount of money, but it was my starting capital, and that was a big lesson for me: *Risky and speculative investments can be fun and exciting, but that doesn't mean you should invest all your money in them.* You should start off with a balanced portfolio and add more speculative options only when you have the money to risk.

LESSON NUMBER 2: Start Investing Early

You should focus on your craft, but also start investing early if you can. One of the best investments you will ever make is in yourself, your practice, or business. It's important that you do not get sidetracked right out of the gate. You must learn how to be a good physician or dentist. You must learn how to manage people. You must learn how to manage patients. You must learn how to manage your practice. You must learn the business (financials, management, marketing, etc.) The list goes on and on because there are so many things that go into building a successful practice.

Invest in yourself and your practice first, then start investing in things that provide passive income. The earlier you start this process the better because compounding interest takes time. Start saving as much as you can (even if it's only a little bit) at age 25 or 30. It's critical to start saving early and to preserve that core principle. If you wait until you're 40 or 50 to start saving—even at much higher rates—you can never make up for that lost time or returns.

LESSON NUMBER 3: Learn About Alternative Investments

Most financial planners traditionally direct their clients to invest in stocks, mutual funds, and bonds. The problem with putting your money into Wall Street is that you have ZERO control over whether the value of a stock rises or falls, which means you have ZERO control over your investment. The performance of the Dow is only slightly related to the financial states of the companies listed. It's affected much more by what's happening in the world, not just in the U.S., but abroad, as well. It's subject to geopolitical strife, third world economics, and a thousand other things, none of which you (and your financial planner) have control over. That's why it's critical that you learn about alternative investments. There are so-called experts, economists, and financial gurus out there who are calling for DOW 50,000 and some calling for DOW 6,000. They can't both be right, and the truth is NOBODY KNOWS what is going to happen in the future. But putting your money into safe investments that you understand makes a lot of sense.

Today my investments are much more about cash flow and much less about speculation. I invest in real estate equity investments, i.e. single and multi-family homes, commercial, and self-storage in good cash flow markets. I also do real estate debt instruments like private lending and notes. I invest in precious metals and cash value life insurance. I still do some investing in stocks, mutual funds, and bonds because there is a place for that type of investment in my portfolio, but you should only do so if you're willing to put in the time and research to understand your own risk tolerance PLUS the present and future needs of your own portfolio.

LESSON NUMBER 4: Tap the Power of the Network

You need to be in a network of like-minded individuals. I've been involved in real estate for twenty years. But like many doctors who dive into real estate, I tried to do it on my own! I had some wins and some losses, and most of the things I was investing in were highly speculative. I didn't really know how to flip that switch and get into the passive income market until I met Dr. David Phelps and became a member of the Freedom Founders Mastermind Community. I plugged into a network of real estate professionals all around the country that gave me access to cash flow investments in lots of different markets rather than just in my own backyard.

You can diversify your risk by investing in different types of markets, different types of neighborhoods, different types of properties— single or multi-family. You can also get into the debt instrument side of investing by becoming the bank and financier of other companies' operations. We also invest in the "paper" side, which means becoming the bank and owning mortgages. There's a lot of diversity that can be created within a single real estate portfolio. Being in a mastermind has been critical to my success, which is why I've started my own mastermind group called, *High Speed Alliance.*

LESSON NUMBER 5: Tax-Free and Tax Efficiency

You should always try to invest in tax-free or tax-efficient environments. Most people have no idea what that even means. Believe me, I'm all for supporting the American Way and strongly believe in our Constitution, lifestyle, and freedom. That means that I want to support the U.S. Government by paying the taxes that I'm required to pay under current federal and state laws. But I don't want to pay any more taxes than required. The Government actually gives us some gifts if you know where to look to decrease your tax burden. One of those gifts involves self-directed Retirement and Health Savings Accounts. Main Street Investors don't know the value of backdoor Roths, HSAs, and Stretch IRAs. Self-directed doesn't mean you select which mutual fund or ETF to purchase from your broker or advisor. This topic is far beyond the scope of this brief chapter, but if you'd like to learn more about tax-free and tax-deferred investments contact me through the HIGH SPEED ALLIANCE website (see the end of this chapter).

LESSON NUMBER 6: Hope for the Future, But Believe in Yourself

Even if you are a hardworking doctor or CEO focusing on your business and your patients, you still must learn these strategies to grow wealth. I'm an optimist in the future, but I've become a Contrarian Investor. Remember the advice about buying low and selling high? Everyone has forgotten that simple truth. You can learn to invest safely and understand what you are doing. You can be in a group that will take you further than you can go on your own. You should be careful if you're putting all your money and trust in the stock market and letting someone else manage your wealth. You're setting yourself up for potential problems. Many Main Street investors are putting too much hope into ETFs. (These are more popular than ever because we have been in a Bull Market - but PLEASE wake up!) There's no better way to learn these investing techniques than joining a great mastermind group and networking with people who already know these strategies inside and out and are willing to teach you. It's like having a dream board of advisors helping you succeed. You can do it, but don't try to go it alone!

LESSON NUMBER 7: Bulletproof Your Practice

You need to "bulletproof" your practice/business against a health catastrophe or a sudden inability to work. Every doctor or dentist, veterinarian, chiropractor, osteopath, etc., needs to have the following three things in place to bulletproof their practice in the event of a catastrophe:

- Individual disability insurance in an amount that's adequate to maintain their lifestyle and income
- Office and overhead insurance to continue to pay the business bills
- Group disability insurance to add an extra layer of protection on top of the individual disability insurance

I call this *The Trifecta of Bulletproofing*. Without these three critical components, you are leaving yourself, your lifestyle, your family, your practice (and patients and employees), and finally, your Legacy at risk.

HIGH SPEED ALLIANCE

High Speed Alliance is a group of doctors, dentists, and small business owners who have teamed up with some of the brightest professionals in various industries: real estate professionals, stock market and insurance specialists, lawyers and accountants, business and marketing coaches, dental and medical gurus. It's like the best board of directors a small business could hope for.

High Speed Alliance provides guidance on how to maximize business revenue and the active income of the CEO. We maximize the active income as it comes into the personal checking account through tax efficiency. Looking at the different savings environments available, we help create a passive income money machine that generates multiple streams of income NOW and in retirement with the goal of achieving passive income that equals or exceeds active income. Doctors and CEOs have an incredible opportunity to generate massive amounts of wealth because of high income and bankability. Sadly, most, don't know how to do this. And so, the law of increasing expenses takes over. If money is in the personal checking account, it will usually be spent frivolously on lifestyle enhancements, not on wealth building. So, by flipping the mentality and teaching doctors what they should do, we can help ensure they make wise decisions and let the dollars work for them.

You must understand this: no one ever got rich with mutual funds. And studies have shown that the wealthier people get, the percentage of mutual funds in their portfolio decreases, i.e. the rich don't let their money sit in mutual funds. Mutual funds were designed for Main Street investors on Wall Street—not for the wealthy.

High Speed Alliance is all about giving CEOs another way to gain education and networking opportunities to learn more about alternative investments. And—depending on the investor—that could be for a good portion of their portfolio or maybe even all their portfolio, depending on their goals. We teach them ways to make tax-free and tax-deferred investments that the mainstream media and Wall Street will never tell you about.

My wife and I have long dreamt of helping our friends and colleagues because we saw so many who were struggling financially (even with a high income). We wanted to teach them what we had discovered. We wanted to help them avoid what I went through when I had my serious health scare. We wanted to teach them how to generate passive income, so that any doctor or CEO could benefit and have less stress and anxiety, better develop dreams and goals, increase their income and their business worth, and create passive income streams that can be reinvested in the business, retirement savings, college savings, or making an impact on causes they care about. That's what creates true freedom and legacy.

Freedom is the ability to do WHAT you want, WHEN you want, WHERE you want, and with WHOM you want. It enables you to take more time off to travel and enjoy life. It lets you work part time in your business if you choose, start another business, or just have the freedom to follow your heart.

Legacy is something that is given to the Living by the Dead. It could be contributing to the long-term benefit of your family, your community, or the causes you care about. Most doctors have big hearts, and they care about their church, charities, communities and schools, disease prevention, and healthcare research. Once freedom is obtained, a legacy can be created that really makes a big difference in these callings.

Luke 12:48 says, "To whom much is given much is expected," and my family and I feel very blessed. We've dealt with and recovered from tremendous setbacks. In my life, the Chinese proverb, "Get knocked down eight times, get up nine" applies.

I just can't quit.

It's my nature to keep charging forward.

We can sleep when we're dead.

In the end, I feel like I can really help others who might be struggling with things like depression, suicide, bankruptcy, decreasing business and personal revenues, divorce, frustration with stock market returns, and uncertain feelings about not having the time to do the things you want to do, like taking family vacations and developing deeper family and friend relationships. For me, not to help is just not an option.

This is just my lifestyle now.

I live to help others learn what I now know.

A good friend of mine says he wants to do three things every day: *do good, make money, and have fun.*

I like that motto.

That's what I do every day, and that's what I want to keep doing.

I want to help people, do good, make money, and have fun. If that sounds interesting to you then please come with us!

For more information on our podcast, blog, newsletter, or upcoming meetings, visit www.highspeedalliance.com.

ABOUT THE AUTHOR

FORREST BRYANT - Growing up, Dr. Bryant wanted to be an astronaut. After entering Auburn University in Aerospace Engineering and seeing the dramatic cutbacks in the Aerospace Industry in the early 1990s, he reignited his eighth grade passion to become a dentist. After graduating from UAB with his dental degree with honors, he and his wife started a family and a career in North Alabama.

He became a partner in his first dental office, and then bought that practice while pursuing continuing dental education and eventually opening two more dental practices. He achieved Fellowship status with the Academy of General Dentistry while contributing to many charities and causes, including foreign dental mission trips. He grew his practice over 500 percent in 15 years to include multiple locations, and multiple doctors and hygienists. Being entrepreneurial, Dr. Bryant wanted to put his business skills to work so he became a dental CEO.

When health problems prevented him from practicing dentistry anymore, Dr. Bryant honed his business skills for several years until he sold the dental practices. He also became a financial advisor for a large investment insurance company, helping high net worth families invest and grow their wealth, as well as protect that wealth against catastrophe.

Dr. Bryant credits Dr. David Phelps with changing his focus on real estate investing from speculative to cash flow. Dr. Bryant learned so much about traditional and alternative investing that he felt compelled to share this knowledge with his peers.

Dr. Bryant and his wife Carol created High Speed Alliance to share their inspiring message of Freedom and Legacy with their peers. The goal of High Speed Alliance is to help create Freedom and Legacy by mastering the business, finances, family, and lifestyle. Dr. Bryant's driving passion is to help others achieve financial freedom and to help them follow their dreams.

Dr. Bryant and his family reside in Huntsville, Alabama, and love to travel, spend time together, and play with their pets.

Contact information:
drb@highspeedalliance.com

Todd Auerbach

DUE DILIGENCE

Our trials are our greatest teachers, mentors and benefactors.
~ Auliq-Ice

My story with real estate begins in 1988, in sunny Southern California. I had just graduated from USC Dental School, May 1987, and was starting my career as a dentist. My goal was to own my own dental practice. I got my chance in 1988 when I was working for a dentist who was suddenly disabled. I offered to buy the practice from her, and she agreed. One dream/goal achieved. As the paperwork for the buy-out was going through, I got engaged. We decided to get married that same year because the number eight is considered very lucky in Chinese culture. How could you go wrong with 88? Also, at that same time came the timing of buying our first house. Buying a practice, getting married, and buying a house, all in one year, was exciting at best. Our first house was a two bedroom, two-and-a-half bath townhouse. This was the start of what everyone tells you when you are growing up, that you should always buy a house, whether it's your starter house or the house that you will live in forever, you should always have a house. It never occurred to me to consider it as a real estate investment.

In 1990, we had our first baby. In 1991, with the impending arrival of baby number two, we decided to try and sell the townhouse while buying a bigger home to accommodate our growing family. This would be the start of our roller coaster ride with real estate. The seller of the house that we were buying, who had just gotten divorced, needed a place to live. Since we were trying to sell our townhouse, he told us that he would buy our townhouse. So, it was to be a sort of trade with an exchange of money on our part, of course. However, it was not to be. At the close of escrow, the seller decided that he would not purchase the townhouse. At this point, we decided to keep the townhouse as a rental. This was our first foray into the land of landlords and property managers. We were landlords to the seller for three months before he purchased another home. So now we had to deal with finding renters. After a few months of having a vacant property, we were able to find new tenants.

For us, being a landlord/property manager only lasted two years. We decided that having a rental property was too much work. So, in 1995, we sold the townhouse at a loss. That was a decision that was hard to swallow. The real estate market in California took a huge dive in values. At the same time, it was a sense of relief not having to worry about the townhouse. Lucky for me as a dentist, I was doing well and able to save money.

As a professional, you attend a lot of seminars. Seminars that will teach you how to improve your practice, for a small fee, or seminars to improve your financial wealth, also for a small fee. The one nugget that I took away from all of this was how to get your money to work for you. Not wanting to spend a lot of time on investments, I put our monthly extra money into buying General/Obligation California Municipal Bonds for tax-free income. Buying these bonds yielded 5% tax-free. I did this for many, many years. As the rates were starting to decline, I was looking into how to diversify our financial portfolio.

Diversifying our portfolio was the start of investment lessons in what not to do. I invested in a company that was buying dental offices in Texas. The premise of this investment was to build a portfolio of dental offices and eventually sell the package to Wall Street. Unfortunately, that did not happen. As more dental practices were purchased, the loan documents took on a subtle change that went unnoticed. In the very, very fine print, it stated that all the dental offices would become collateral for each other instead of being held as an individual practice. Added to that, a dentist that was managing one of the practices was embezzling, and the bank that held the note for all of the practices was forced to foreclose on all of the dental offices. That was a very, very expensive lesson for me.

My next investment was in real estate, but without having to do any actual work. It was putting private money into a fund that would find property, all cash, in Texas. The cash flow was good for a while, BUT after not receiving regular payments from the fund, something was starting to look suspicious. All the investors found out that the person in charge of the fund took out a loan on all the properties. Twenty-one properties were in that portfolio. The loan used the twenty-one properties as collateral, and he invested the money in a stock WITHOUT approval from the investors. The fund eventually declared bankruptcy. The bank that held the loan had a prepayment clause and was forced to foreclose on all the properties. All the investors ended up receiving less than $0.10 on the dollar that was invested. Yes, that was another very, very expensive lesson for me. My money was definitely not working for me.

You would think that after all of this, I would be shy about any more investing, but sadly, no. So, at this point in our lives, our four kids were almost all adults, and my wife discovered HGTV. She's always been kind of handy and really liked watching those home improvement shows. *LOVE IT OR LIST IT, PROPERTY BROTHERS, INCOME PROPERTY, FLIP OR FLO.* She was hooked and got a bug that she wanted to try to flip a house. She heard about a free seminar that would teach you how to find, buy and flip a house for a profit. There was even an HGTV celebrity there to talk about how he started in real estate. We went to the seminar together and were amazed at the knowledge that they shared. We signed up for the classes that would teach us how to do this. They taught good principles in what to look for. Invest in working neighborhoods. The houses should be at least three bedrooms, two baths, and we should make sure that the property, after expenses, would be cash flowing. They imparted that buying out of state, meaning anywhere but California, would be a good idea. BUT it didn't end there. They also have a seminar that they call a "Buying Summit." This seminar that is held in Las Vegas gives you the opportunity to buy turnkey properties for wholesale prices. They had vetted everything for you. There were renters in the properties, and the property managers had been vetted for you, but you could always change the property management company if you chose to do so. They also had another HGTV celebrity there to share their real estate story. This company also had notes that could be purchased as well as vacant land parcels that were ready to be built on.

So, while being at this "Buying Summit," we thought it was a great concept. We could buy property, have the property management company that came with it continue to manage it as well as having a tenant already in the property that was cash flowing. What a no-brainer, right? For the first few months, everything was great. Then a vacancy in one of the properties and then another. That is when we discovered that our rental properties were not in working class neighborhoods, but they were in borderline war zones. The lesson that we learned ... DUE DILIGENCE is important as well as vetting the company that you deal with and staying away from anything connected to real estate and HGTV celebrities.

This brings us to where we are now. I responded to an email from Freedom Founders (Dr. David Phelps) discussing Plan B. Plan B is designed to create your passive income for when you want to retire and still maintain the style of living that you are accustomed to or want. To have the freedom to do what you want, when you want and with whom you want. We went to a meeting in Dallas. You would think that we would want to stay out of anything that had to do with Texas with our past history, but we went anyway. This meeting was a game changer for us, and it was the BEST thing we ever did. Surrounding yourself with like-minded people is an amazing phenomenon. At this meeting, we talked with other people in the group that had been with them for a while. We talked with real estate people that were there. This time around, we were more cautious of investing. After almost a year of observing and checking on deals that came through this group, we started to invest our money in various real estate opportunities. We started with lending positions—short-term lending deals. Those short-term lending deals paid what was promised. Feeling more confident, we decided to move forward. We have now invested in some turnkey rental properties that are cash flowing. Currently, we have properties in five different states, some joint ventures with other members, and are doing lending deals secured by real estate.

After everything that we have been through and the amount of money that has been lost, it's really, really nice to be a part of a group that doesn't judge but has the same goals that you do. We trust these people and continue our journey with confidence as we find our financial freedom.

ABOUT THE AUTHOR

TODD AUERBACH - Yes, that's me, Todd Auerbach. I'm a general dentist in Orange County. When I was in eighth grade, I decided that I wanted to be a dentist. That dream motivated me to finish high school in three years and then go on to the University of Southern California (USC). I also had the privilege of attending dental school AT USC, FIGHT ON! As a general dentist, I love doing cosmetic dentistry, orthodontics, treating TMJ and sleep apnea. It's a pleasure not only to give my patients the beautiful smile that they want but help them achieve total body wellness.

Finding Financial Freedom has taken a huge weight off my shoulders, and I hope it can do the same for you.

Brad Burau

LIFE IS ABOUT THE JOURNEY
...NOT THE DESTINATION

THE STATION
By Robert J. Hastings

Tucked away in our subconscious is an idyllic vision.
We are traveling by train, out the windows,
we drink in the passing scenes of children
waving at a crossing,
cattle grazing on a distant hillside,
row upon row of corn and wheat,
flatlands and valleys,
mountains and rolling hillsides
and city skylines.
But uppermost in our minds is the final destination.
On a certain day, we will pull into the station.
Bands will be playing and flags waving.
Once we get there, our dreams will come true
And the pieces of our lives
will fit together like a completed jigsaw puzzle.
Restlessly we pace the aisles,
Damning the minutes-waiting,
Waiting, waiting for the station.
When we reach the station, that will be it!"

We cry, "When I'm 18." "When I buy a new 450sl Mercedes Benz!"
"When I put the last kid through college."
"When I have paid off the mortgage!"
"When I get a promotion."
"When I reach retirement, I shall live happily ever after!"
Sooner or later, we realize there is no station.
No one place to arrive. The true joy of life is the trip.
The station is only a dream.
It constantly outdistances us.
"Relish the moment" is a good motto.
It isn't the burdens of today that drive men mad.
It is the regrets over yesterday and the fear of tomorrow.
Regret and fear are twin thieves who rob us of today.
Regret is reality, after the facts.
So stop pacing the aisles and counting the miles.
Instead, climb more mountains, eat more ice cream,
Go barefoot more often,
Swim more rivers, watch more sunsets, laugh
More cry less.
Life must be lived as we go along.
The STATION will come soon enough

* * *

I believe life is really all about the journey and not the destination. Too many of us focus only on the end result and not the process. To achieve success in life, one has to be goal oriented with expected outcomes, while including enjoyment along the way. Life is like a quest. Each of us is like his or her own Christopher Columbus…searching and exploring new worlds.

Ah, so this is where it gets interesting. How are we supposed to have fun and goals if we don't know what they are or what we are working for? And here is my point … all of us started out after school "young and dumb." I graduated from dental school, got married to my wife and best friend of thirty years, Mary Yana, bought a car, went on a honeymoon cruise, moved into an apartment (interest rates were 15%), and started work, all within a month of leaving school. Boy, there's not a lot of time for planning and thinking about retirement in that short time. My wife had to make my first car payment before we were married because I was without money. Were they really serious about us paying before the due date? I had so much to do.

So you see, most of us are so busy with our lives, and the important people involved, that our focus on saving and planning for the future usually gets put off, whether we try to or not. So, fast forward six months to a lazy Saturday. We think my wife is pregnant, so off to the drugstore to get a pregnancy test. The first test is positive; however, it's been several years since I had chemistry. So, back to the drugstore to get another test we go. As I'm testing the second time (remember we were taught in dental school "Always check twice"), I again confirm the pink color as positive. From the family room my wife asks, "How pink is it?" "Very," I responded. So now begins parenthood, and again, where is the time, extra money, or inclination to work on your plan B or retirement?

So my point in depicting these stories for our readers is this … Most of us had little time, money, or reason to think or worry about retirement. And beyond that, we probably couldn't tell each other what it meant or what we actually wanted in retirement. I'm illustrating these points to show everyone with similar stories that this whole "Plan B" or retirement plan really is a "process," or a journey. It's not until we reach a certain age or maturity before we can actually figure out what we want our lives to be like, at or during retirement.

A wise man once said, "Begin with the end in mind." If this could be done at the beginning of working, that would be ideal; however, few if any have the time and foresight to accomplish this. My solution is this: "Begin with the end in mind" when you have been on the journey long enough to know what the end could look like. As you are on your journey, remember you have to really enjoy what you are doing. And what I mean by that is whatever steps you take in real estate investing, make sure you enjoy the process. Many different paths are illustrated in this book. Some will be appealing and others will not. Be open and try different things so you can find your method to successful investing. No two paths will be the same, but all the paths will eventually lead to a similar end point. And remember, some things will work better than others. Finally, a good journey is not a perfect journey. Enjoy the highs and lows in this journey we are all on towards a successful retirement, or "Plan B."

Mary Yana and I came to our first Mastermind in May of 2015. And like many of you would feel in a new situation around some very intelligent people, we were somewhat intimidated. What were they talking about? It seemed like a different language. What's a wrap? How can you just wire someone money and send a note? Isn't that something only the mortgage people and banks do? You can buy how many houses with a mortgage? Our heads were spinning. Was this the right place for us? After six months, we finally became more comfortable. We began to understand the brainwashing that Wall Street had perpetrated on all of us. We learned that we could all help each other toward financial freedom instead of helping Wall Street. Above all, we could do it with nice people who were honest and had integrity. When I looked back on my experience with Wall Street, I was entrusting my money to managers whom I didn't know. Did they share my values? Did they care about my money? The most important detail when investing are the people you invest with. My question to all of you is "Why not do business with good people who you know have integrity?" Business sense is important too, as all of our dealings have been conducted with the notion to "trust and confirm." Paperwork and legal documents have always been notarized and signed to protect all parties.

Six months later, Mary Yana and I participated in our first deal. We started out lending. These were simple deals and got us comfortable with the process. I personally enjoy the house rental side of the real estate business. Having only one of our three children left at home, we had the time to acquire twelve rental properties in the last year. It was quite a project, but very rewarding. The main advantage I see is that there is a substantial depreciation component, which helps offset income on a W-2 form. This is appealing to me because of my continued work in the dental field. Secondly, it's appealing to have a business besides dentistry which affords business expenses. So, for those two reasons, and my enjoyment of the process and challenge, our real estate venture has become the mainstay of our retirement plan, or "Plan B."

My hope for readers is that they receive an insight into the process and struggles that my wife and I have gone through in breaking free of the chains of Wall Street. I hope that our readers realize the time it takes to evaluate and comprehend what one's definition of retirement is, and how it relates to one's freedom. Humor aside … life, liberty, and the pursuit of a retirement plan can really be an adventure. It should be enjoyed with great people who you can partner with for mutual success. But most of all, it's a journey full of ups and downs. It's a journey full of learning. It's a journey that will take you places and have you doing things you never thought possible. And finally, when you do reach THE STATION, you will look back and appreciate the journey.

ABOUT THE AUTHOR

BRAD BURAU - My story begins long before dental school. I have always had an entrepreneurial lean to my thinking. I learned very early that one always finds more success working for oneself than someone else. At the age of ten, I began a lawn business, which eventually grew to more than thirteen lawns a week. I made an incredible amount of money for a young kid and learned a great deal about people and business. However, this business was labor intensive and required my time and energy to make it run, which is usually the way things are at the start. Time and sweat are traded for dollars.

As I grew older, I was able to acquire a job at one of the nearby General Motors Plants. Ironically, one of my lawn business customers was a plant manager. He knew my work ethic and hired me. I worked for three summers at the GM plant. Long hours were a given as I began work at 6:30 am and worked until 5:30 pm on the weekdays. Fortunately, they gave me some time off on Saturdays and Sunday, when I only had to be there from 6:00 am to 2:00 pm. This experience only served to solidify the initial impressions I had as a ten-year-old. I really preferred working for myself! My experience at GM that I was grateful to have, shaped my underlying thinking concerning work, life and freedom.

During this time, I became interested in windsurfing; however, I could not afford a windsurf because they were $1,500 at the time. Ironically, I heard that a camp in northern Michigan was selling six windsurfs and was negotiable on the price. After calling and talking to the camp director, my entrepreneurial spirit was kindled as they were desperate to sell all six. I convinced my dad to loan me the van, and I made the four-hour trip north. I left with my checkbook showing a balance of $1,500, which was my entire life savings. That night, I arrived home with six complete windsurfs and a big zero in my checkbook. Six hours of driving had produced an opportunity for me. I was able to sell all six windsurfs, purchase the one I wanted ($1,500), and still have a couple of thousand dollars profit. Incidentally, this was the money I later spent on my wife's wedding ring while I was a junior in dental school. My wife always loves this story. This was my first lesson in "thinking outside of the box."

Fast forward now to life after dental school. I had just completed the "dreaded" four years, and I was now ready to be a "real" person. My wife and I were married, and I began my career with my dad in Grand Blanc, Michigan. Fortunately, my dad was very supportive and an excellent mentor at the office. Although I began the "grind" with the help of an experienced and knowledgeable dentist, I would make some mistakes. Stocks and investing were of interest, and I quickly tried to learn as much as I could, including watching Louis Rukeyser (a weekly investment show) and reading many books. My brother, Scott, who is my partner at the dental office, and I even went to investment conferences to try to get an "edge" in investing.

I had some successes and some failures. I made some good profitable investments and some poor ones. I remember when the big screen TVs came out, and I had to have one. I thought, "if I bought a particular stock and it went up … I could get one for free!" Well, that didn't work, and the company's stock eventually went bankrupt. I sold it only after losing potentially four TVs. The light was flickering, but had not fully turned on in my head yet.

So, I got a financial advisor like most "successful" people do, and started on the path to "saving for retirement." This is where I may differ with many in this book. Benefitting from the services of an ethical firm providing assistance for over eighteen years, I have only paid .5-1% /year of my portfolio value as compensation for all the advice and legal accounting work. I felt that I received fair and ethical advice and guidance. Here, it was important that both parties were looking for the same thing in the relationship. If I was successful and the value of my portfolio went up, we both made money.

There were, however, a few major caveats I experienced with stock investing. The first is volatility. I was with money managers who had carte blanche with our money. They were like small hedge funds. In good times, I was hugely up, and in bad times, in the "wrong direction." Wild swings between years were the norm. Secondly, I was always paying large capital gains from my dental income in "the good years." I felt I had to keep the gains compounding. Although this was perhaps a good theory, it put a strain on my daily life and earned income. It was really frustrating to pay capital gains from my wages, only to see my portfolio value shrink the next year wiping out the gains I had just paid for with taxes. It was up, and it was down. Lastly, it felt like you were only living for a number on a piece of paper. The government scalped large chunks from the non-IRA investments, and I was stuck paying huge fees to the actuary for the retirement plan.

Then came the stock market crash of 2008. Literally, half of our portfolio was wiped off the map. Most people panicked. Many people withdrew all of their money from the stock market. My advisor was patient and ended up giving me some good advice. I stayed the course and recouped most of the lost investment, but what a ride. It made me begin to wonder if there was a better way?

I believe I was lucky at this time. Unlike some, I was not ready to retire. I was coaching tennis and looking at colleges for my kids. My family life was busy, and I was distracted. So for many reasons, my decision was based more on "Oh well, I don't have the time to worry about it." Quite obviously and retrospectively, this does not show a great deal of wisdom and reflection on my part; however as the year 2015 approached, I finally awakened from my "nightmare in fantasy land." My brother and dental partner came to me and said, "I'm going to this conference to join a Mastermind Group. Do you want to come?" We've been partners for twenty-five years, and there is a lot of trust between us. My reply was "yes," and thus, my path to freedom through real estate was born. It has placed us on a firm pathway to sound retirement potential.

Contact information:
drbburau@yahoo.com

Scott Burau

THE COLLEGE VISIT:
or how to count your chickens
before they hatch

"**W**ait for it...wait for it."

My wife, Lisa, and I have been through this before. We were at one of those college walking tours with our son, Adam. They're usually given by a hyper-motivated young student who has a little extra time, has lots of motivation, and needs to make a little money. As we were walking around campus on a beautiful day, seeing how cool this building is and how totally awesome the food is there, inevitably one person asks that all-important question that everyone's trying to avoid: How much does it cost to go to school here?!

The student was well trained and didn't miss a beat. With a quick smile, his response was this: "Well, it's $42,000, but ALMOST NO-BODY pays that." We heard a smattering of uncomfortable laughs (probably mine), and then we were off to see this place where all the sorority girls hang out.

Well, I'd like to introduce us. We are Mr. and Mrs. Almost Nobody. That's right, we pay full price. No scholarships or grants. FAFSA, the government's college financial aid form, has determined that we should pay it ALL.

There is a segment of people who aren't necessarily millionaires, but can't qualify for the available need-based scholarships and grants. Compounding this is having more than one kid to educate. Now don't get me wrong. I'm more than willing to pay my fair share, but it seems that if you qualify for financial aid, there is a lot of help out there to make sure you get through the process and get the most out of it. However, if you're in our shoes, there aren't too many people talking about the best way to afford college or how to best pay for college. We've saved since before the kids were born, however, no one prepared us for these kinds of numbers.

Our pathway to doing this was to combine college savings plans with any money we are saving for retirement, place it in various, more aggressive stock funds and direct management funds, because we had a long-term time horizon in which to invest this money. The conventional wisdom then was before you start to need it, put it in investments that are more conservative, and then start pulling it out of the account.

Oh, and as we discovered, college savings plans like 529s, etc., help build those funds, but also mark you as a target on the FAFSA as someone who can afford to pay more for college.

As we looked into paying for college, it was painful to think about taking out that much capital on a yearly basis from the account and losing its earning power. $42,000 the first and second years, and $84,000 after that—my daughter was next.

I didn't want to leave my kids with this much debt, but I knew I needed the income that this money would produce in my retirement. I didn't want to deplete the savings that had taken twenty years to build up in the account. The earning power of this money was too great to just take it out of the account and spend. There had to be a better way.

I needed help and advice from someone who wasn't going to just replay the usual conventional wisdom, i.e., Wall Street: "Put your money into the market and hope it goes up. And, by the way, make sure the nest egg number is super big, or college costs could eat up your whole retirement." That philosophy works if the stock market keeps going up and if you invest enough to get a big enough nest egg by the time you need the money.

The problem is that hasn't happened. Not only from the standpoint of the quantity of money saved, but also, as anyone can see by looking at their own accounts, Wall Street just hasn't held up its end of the bargain. And many pedants really don't predict good years to come in the next decade.

So where do I find this advice? I started to do a lot of reading about investing and real estate, and how to start into that uncharted territory. One such book kept talking about having some trusted advisers or a Board of Directors. We don't know what we don't know. This group of specialized knowledgeable people can tell you what you don't know. The book introduced me to the term Mastermind Meeting. Napoleon Hill, author of *Think and Grow Rich*, defined a mastermind group as "The coordination of knowledge and effort of two or more people, who work toward a definite purpose, in the spirit of harmony." This sounded like a great way of problem solving. Many minds helping me solve my problem, and my mind helping someone else solve theirs. The book discussed joint ventures. It talked about private real estate lending and turnkey rentals. I had never heard of these terms before. I was intrigued, so I went to a Mastermind meeting to learn.

At the first meeting, I met someone whose interesting philosophy changed my outlook forever. His comment was simply "Quit buying eggs and start buying chickens." That simple statement had a profound impact on my thinking, not only about this college experience, but also, my life in general. If I could buy "a chicken" that would generate money on a monthly and yearly basis, I could use that to pay the college expenses. Then, at the end of the deal, I could still use the chicken to help take care of financial needs in our later years, when we got to retirement. This sounded like what I was looking for, so we applied and got federal student loans.

As an interesting side note, when we were notified by the school that the documents were ready to sign, the school made sure to tell us our AWARD was ready to accept! It wasn't an award just like our mortgage isn't an award. It's a loan we went out and found that must be repaid! Not something the school did for us ... (breathe, breathe...)

So, the plan is to purchase an asset or group of assets (chickens) that can generate the cash flow (eggs) needed to make the payment on the college loans. There are many ways to do this. We do it by purchasing turnkey rental properties that cash flow monthly. We use this cash flow to pay the College AWARD—I mean loan payments. These properties are managed by a company. We don't do toilets or tenants. That's part of the joint venture. At the end, the money we would have spent for college will still be available to produce an income when we retire.

Connecting with the Mastermind Group has given me knowledge about the many real estate investment opportunities available and the network of trusted individuals to help us without having to reinvent the wheel by learning everything about real estate acquisition financing and management. This is important because I have a regular job, and I don't have time for a second job. I feel confident and comfortable today because I have a very real and possible way to win this game—and keep my chickens!

ABOUT THE AUTHORS

SCOTT BURAU - I grew up in a family heavily influinfluenced by dentistry and the University of Michigan. Mom and Dad met at the University of Michigan School of Dentistry, where mom was the president of her dental hygiene class and dad was a student in the dental school. I wasn't forced into the family trade. It just felt natural. When I graduated from dental school in 1990, my older brother, Brad, was already a member of my dad's practice in Grand Blanc, Michigan. Also, my younger brother, Keith, was in college, soon to become the fourth dentist in the family, all graduates of the U of M. People say my sister Kathryn was the sane one. She didn't become a dentist. However, she did work on the business side of the practice for a few years before working for a dental supply company in Chicago and starting a family.

Currently, I have been married to Lisa for twenty-four years. We have three children. Our son Adam is in his second year in college, and our daughter, Ellie, will be starting college this coming fall, hence the need to figure out how to finance college. Our youngest daughter, Lucy, will be in her second year of high school.

The secret to our family's success is really quite simple. It involves a combination of four core values. First, we have and practice a very strong Christian faith, regularly within our family and out in public. Second, we have very tight family relationships, and our children know this is vitally important to our success and is second only to our relationship with our Creator. Third, a good education and the idea of being a life-long student are critical in order to reach one's goals. Finally, hard work completes the list. This is important whether it is in the classroom or on the tennis court. We are always focused on doing the best we can in any given situation.

These core values have shaped my family and me for my entire life. These didn't come from me, but have been passed from previous generations to the new ones. I am standing on the shoulders of giants! I believe that if these core values are really lived, happiness, life fulfillment, and financial freedom (this book) are a natural result. My main goal in life is to pass this philosophy on to my children, so that, most importantly, they are ready to meet God. Additionally, I want them to be able to attain success and pass these core values on to their children.

Contact information:
sburau@mac.com
mobile phone 810-444-1143

William Caldon

LEARNING FROM OTHER PEOPLE'S MISTAKES— NAMELY MINE

We have all heard the adage that states that experience is the best teacher. That may indeed be true; however, experience may also be the most painful teacher. My wife Margaret likes to refer to the resources expended and the physical and emotional pain endured as the result of experiential misadventures as tuition. In the next few paragraphs, I hope to convey to you some of the tuition we have paid in regards to our investing in the hopes that you can learn from our mistakes and avoid some of the tuition that you might otherwise have to expend.

Paying this real world tuition on more than one occasion can make you a more effective teacher or mentor. Our oldest son Josh is an Air Force pilot, and he would be the first to tell you that he is not a natural pilot. Consequently, he has had to learn to fly by sometimes making mistakes (fortunately all very survivable). This learning process has made him a very effective instructor pilot. Whereas the natural pilots cannot understand, much less anticipate, the mistakes the student pilot makes, Josh is in a great position to anticipate and understand the mistakes that the student pilots might make because he has already made most of them himself. My hope is that in reading these stories, you will learn from my mistakes and not have to experience them yourself. Tuition can indeed be painful. Let me add that these misadventures are mine and mine alone, and my dear wife Margaret has been unbelievably tolerant and loving, as I have blundered my way through these often ill-conceived forays into the unknown for the last wonderful forty-two years.

In any investment there is an array of questions that you should ask yourself regarding that investment. I'll take you through these questions and relate to you how I have in the past disregarded the ramifications of those questions, and also I will discuss some of the resulting consequences we have suffered. To be fair, not all of the decisions I have made have been disastrous. The following are merely some of the lowlights:

1. The first question you need to ask is **Do I understand the investment?** Unfortunately, I have several examples of how I have disregarded this, not understanding what I didn't know. One incident is the commercial building that I purchased with two other partners, which houses our dental practice. It is a two-story, 25,000 square foot building with the 15,000 square foot first floor partially rented and a 10,000 square foot upper level that is completely undeveloped. We figured that we could afford the $1.4 million purchase price and the $750,000 renovation price tag if the dental practice took over half of the upper space and we were able to get a few more rentals, because as we all know "If you build it, they will come." Nearly five years later, the property remains under-rented and the commercial bank loan has a five-year bubble. With the income to debt ratio being less than what the bank requires, they are likely to call in the loan in a few months, which is a frightening proposition. It's not as if many people are able to come up with $1.5 million in liquid assets no matter how many couch cushions they turn over.

2. The next question you need to ask is **Do I know and trust the peo-**

ple involved in the deal? This is probably my biggest downfall. I am an inherently trusting individual and seem to have trouble doing some simple things to overcome this weakness—a repeat offender, so to speak. Fool me once, shame on you. Fool me twice, shame on me. Trust is not necessarily a bad thing, but as Ronald Reagan said in his dealings with the Soviet Union, we need to "Trust **AND VERIFY.**" Sometimes a simple Google of the individual will reveal a wealth of information. I have joint ventured with a trainer who sold my racehorses without permission and pocketed $40,000. I have partnered with a dentist who was a recalcitrant alcoholic with a low work ethic and no leadership ability, who ran one of our offices completely into the ground. The coup de grace was when I hired a young man as CFO who went to school with and grew up with our children, yet still managed to embezzle $400,000 from us. I have also been lucky enough to have done some deals that I did not understand with some extremely wonderful and honest individuals who have taken great care of me, in spite of my ignorance.

3. Which leads me to the next question **If I do not understand the investment completely, is the individual who I am joint venturing with a trustworthy expert with a proven track record?** It was probably not a good idea (as my depleted bank account affirmed) for me to invest in oil platform managing ships and real estate development deals that were directed by an accounting firm. Obvious to me now, and should have been at the time, those deals were not exactly in their wheelhouse. A corollary to this advice is to beware of joint ventures with someone named Madoff. Fortunately I managed to avoid that one.

4. The next questions are related to one another. **What is the best**

thing that could happen with the investment? What is the worst thing that could happen with the investment? And finally, If the worst thing happens, what impact will it have on my life? Obviously, the critical questions are regarding the worst things and their impact on your life. For an extreme example, if the potential upside of the deal is a gain of $1 million—and the potential loss is $10,000, which may not have a devastating impact on your overall portfolio—this would quite likely be a tolerable risk. However, as I stated in reference to the commercial building that houses our dental practice, if the upside of the deal is potential future appreciation of the building and some cash flow when the building is fully rented versus the downside of having the bank call the $1.5 million loan backed by personal assets if the building is not fully rented, the answer now seems pretty obvious. If I had understood and appreciated the risks I was taking in the purchase of the building, I would never have become involved under those terms.

5. The next question is **Does the investment align with my core values?** Knowing the full extent of the deal is critical when making this determination. For example, if you were a believer in humans being responsible for climate change, would you want to invest in an industry in China that caused unfettered pollution? Or if you were an active member of PETA, would you invest in a mink farm? Unlikely. Another thing to consider is whether all parties involved in the investment benefit from the deal. With real estate as an example, could you sleep at night if you thought that the tenants of your properties were not living in safe and healthy conditions? Fortunately, this is not a mistake that I have made to my knowledge. Even the horse trainer that was stealing from me was at least taking

good care of the animals. I might add that there should be no reason why being involved in the investment can't be fun. If you're not enjoying yourself doing it, it probably is not completely in line with your core values.

6. Another thing to consider is **What effect will the investment have on my cash flow?** The deal may have all of the upsides in the world with almost no risk, but if it leaves you without enough available cash to support your lifestyle, it probably shouldn't be one that you want to pursue. One example of how this has impacted Margaret and me is our 401(k)s. In his book *Killing Sacred Cows*, Garrett Gunderson completely debunks the myth of how a 401(k) sets you up for those golden retirement years. The problems with a 401(k) are many, to which I can personally attest. The idea is that in a 401(k) your money can grow tax-deferred until you decide to use the funds in those retirement years when you are in a lower tax bracket. So, as you are investing in the 401(k), you are doing this at the expense of immediate reduced cash flow to create a bolus of funds to live off in retirement. First of all, as we mature, do we actually want to be in a lower tax bracket? Maybe. But in reality, wouldn't it be okay if our income in retirement was just as healthy as when we were working full-time? Also, isn't it likely that actual tax rates are going to increase as we mature? In addition, none of us knows the exact date and time that we will be called to meet our Maker, so how do we know if we have enough funds stored away to take us to the end? Also, do we want to reduce our existing lifestyles to give us a better chance to have the money last long enough, or would we rather use our newfound retirement free time to do more fun things? Finally, you are limited by the directions put forth by the 401(k) on how

you can invest proceeds in the fund. For example, Margaret cannot invest in real estate in her 401(k), and the only ways she can access the funds to do so are:

1.) Take a distribution and pay taxes at a normal income rate
2.) Turn 65
3.) Quit her job

My business's 401(k) also will not let me invest my funds in real estate, and so I have opted to close the fund so that I can roll the proceeds into a self-directed IRA. The way our 401(k) is set up, it is going to take me eighteen months to close it and access those funds. So what if the funds are fully invested in the stock market and the market makes one of its cyclical corrections? Can your lifestyle survive a 50% cut in available money? Finally, as the owner and trustee of the 401(k), I am fiscally responsible to the other investors for the activity of the fund, something that is way out of my expertise and comfort level, even though I have professional plan administrators and attorneys to supposedly protect me.

7. Another thing to consider in your investments is **Are there any hidden costs?** In our 401(k), there is a 1% management fee, which may not seem like much but can be devastating in a flat stock market like we've had for the last fifteen years, or even worse, in a downturn. In real estate investments, all costs need to be considered: fixed vs variable rates if you've used bank financing, insurance, maintenance, management fees, vacancies, homeowner association fees, realty fees, etc.

8. We have talked about risk consideration in an investment. Another question to ask is **Is there a way I can transfer any of the risk?** One

of the major ways to do this is with insurance. Insurance is typically a relatively low cost way to shift your risk to a company that mitigates its risk by distributing it over a large portion of the population. As a simple example, for a $50,000 single family home, you can insure it against fire for a few hundred dollars per year. For a minimal amount of cash you have protected your asset by transferring that risk to the insurance company. Garrett Gunderson is a strident advocate of insuring investments to the maximum amount affordable and pooh-poohs the idea of self-insurance. To self-insure the aforementioned $50,000 dwelling, you would have to have that $50,000 readily available which takes it out of the pool of money available for other investments. We went to repair the deck surrounding our home only to discover that it was poorly attached to the house, which resulted in about $100,000 of uninsured water damage. In retrospect, a simple analysis of our homeowner's policy might have saved us a great deal of this unexpected expense for which we had not self-insured.

9. Time is a finite entity, so we need to ask ourselves **How much time is the investment going to take, and do I have that time?** With mortgage rates being at an all-time historical low, in an effort to speed the growth of our real estate portfolio, Margaret and I decided to use bank financing to purchase investment properties in our self-directed IRAs, against the recommendations of some trusted advisers. Using bank funding is time consuming and doing so within an IRA adds another time-munching layer of complexity. In six of the nine deals that we tried to consummate, after going through the massive amount of time-consuming paperwork, the deals fell through when the appraisal came in too low. In one of those deals, after we had

completed all of the paperwork for a duplex that was being purchased as separate units within each of our IRAs, the seller decided to combine the two units into one single unit forcing us to repeat all of the paperwork. After doing the paperwork for the second time, the appraisals came in too low, and the deal fell through. We are now using another lender for the same deal, so we are going through the paperwork for the third time. Still being the main chairside producer in my dental practice and Margaret being a full-time nurse, in retrospect, I should have trusted my advisers and found a less time-consuming way to invest our IRA funds. I did not foresee what a huge time-sink this way of investing would have become.

A common theme through these nine mistakes that I have made is that I have either not involved myself with experts whom I could trust, I trusted people I should not have, or I have foolishly disregarded the counsel of trusted experts who were giving me sound advice. As Porter Gale states in his bestselling book *Your Net Worth is Your Network:* "I believe that your 'net worth' will be based not on the size of your portfolio, but on your ability to define and stay true to your passions and values and that working with other people who share them will allow you to build a strong and enduring safety net that will carry you through any financial calamity to greater output and personal fulfillment."

Margaret and I have involved ourselves in Masterminds with extremely knowledgeable, high integrity people who in many cases have also paid their tuition through mistakes that they have made. They continue to teach us the subtleties and nuances of real estate investing that can provide high level, safe and predictable returns in any type of market climate. This network we have become a part of puts us in an excellent position to pass this knowledge on to you, the novice investor, so that you may avoid the tuition some of us have already paid.

As you go forward, I hope that this baring of my investor soul will be of assistance to you in your own investments so that you do not make some of the same ill-conceived blunders I have made. Best of luck to you in all of your future endeavors, and may the force of good relationships be with you.

ABOUT THE AUTHOR

DOCTOR BILL CALDON is a well-recognized clinician, lecturer, educator and best-selling author. He grew up in northern Kentucky across the Ohio River from Cincinnati, and after graduating from high school at the age of fifteen, he received his Bachelor of Arts degree in biology from Thomas More College in 1972. After Dr. Caldon received his Doctor of Dental Medicine degree from the University of Louisville in 1976 as the youngest graduate in his class, he served in the United States Air Force for twenty years, retiring as a full Colonel.

During his distinguished military career, he received training in an arduous two-year general dentistry residency and successfully challenged the demanding Federal Services Board of General Dentistry being recognized by the military as a specialist in general dentistry. For the maximum three years, he served as only one of three Air Force dentists as an examiner on that Federal Services Board. As an instructor in an Advanced Education Program in General Dentistry, he taught recent dental graduates courses in the disciplines of restorative dentistry, pediatric dentistry, temporomandibular joint disorders, orthodontics, and oral pathology. For three years, he served as the director of a one-year general dentistry residency and commanded Air Force dental clinics in England, New York, and New Jersey.

In 2013, Dr. Caldon received the coveted Quilly award from the National Academy of Best Selling Authors for coauthoring the book, *Out Front: Business Building Strategies from Front Line Entrepreneurs*, a collection of advice and success stories from several accomplished business people, which made the Amazon Best Seller list. His television interview regarding the success of the book and his business achievements has been seen on ABC, CBS, NBC and CNBC affiliates across the country. He has been quoted as a premier expert in dentistry in USA TODAY, and he has been featured on over 300 nationally recognized websites such as Reuters, Market Watch, and Yahoo Finance.

In 2014, he received a second Quilly award for coauthoring another best-selling book, *Breaking Through*, with one of his all-time heroes, Dr. Nido Qubein. In addition, he received the distinguished Expy Award in 2014 from the prestigious National Association of Experts, Writers and Speakers for his expertise in media and communications.

Along with his partner Dr. Mike O'Connor, Dr. Caldon helps direct a thriving general dentistry practice in Plattsburgh, New York, on the shores of beautiful Lake Champlain. He is a Fellow in the Academy of General Dentistry, a Diplomate in the American Board of General Dentistry, and is a member of the International College of Dentistry, the American Association of Implantology, and the American Dental Association. He possesses certificates in Oral Conscious Sedation, Invisalign (invisible braces orthodontics), and Short Term Orthodontics. He routinely achieves over 100 hours of continuing education each year.

Dr. Caldon is married to Margaret, his childhood sweetheart and bride of over forty years. Margaret has a Bachelor of Science degree in mathematics from Northern Kentucky State University and uses her

RN degree to serve as a nurse in a local private pediatric office. They have four very successful children, each of whom is either on active duty in the military or is serving in the Air National Guard. They have eight simply incredible grandchildren.

Contact information:
caldonwilliam@gmail.com
www.HighPeaksDental.com

Gerry J. Casazza

A SHIFT IN MINDSET

All of us, whether we be doctors, lawyers, professional business owners, or working people are so consumed with working that we don't spend any time on strategically planning how to get wealthy.

The notion of getting a good education, a great job with benefits, and working hard so you can retire is NOT a plan! While noble, it does not create financial freedom. It only assures a job for the rest of your life.

The mindset for most of my career was to work really, really hard and put in very long hours at the office with the hope that someday this would lead to financial freedom. I had the mindset to go it alone. The belief that I, as a business owner, was smart enough to figure stuff out myself. I also mistakenly believed I had to know everything before I could make a decision and take action. The fact is you will NEVER know it all. This very fact will paralyze you from ever taking the massive actions necessary for true success.

For most of my life, I had no clue about making money. Even though I owned and managed two very profitable dental practices, at the end of the day I was so busy earning a living I made no time for money. My work became my life!

Even on Sundays I found the need to be at the office to address the things that did not get done during the week. This period in my life lasted more than twenty years!

It was not until late in my career that I realized there was more to running a successful business than simply knowing your trade (whatever that is) and having employees. A successful business, in my opinion, is defined as one that can run itself and be truly profitable without the owner actively trading time for dollars.

Fortunately, it was by associating with highly successful mentors, coaches, and business people that put me on the fast track to financial freedom. I modeled their behavior and habits. I surrounded myself with fewer and better people who had already achieved in their life what I was looking to achieve. The key, I found, is to surround yourself with intelligent people and leverage their time, skills, knowledge, and experience. This will certainly fast track your results better than anything you can do by yourself.

Today my approach to financial freedom is threefold:

FIRST, it's all about generating income. Income can be either active or passive.

Active income is generated through capital assets such as real businesses. Again, I define a real business as one that is not dependent on your active labor to produce that income. You can choose to be involved as much as you want, but the business (whatever that is) is able to run itself through proven systems and proper management.

Passive income is usually received with little effort or time on your part. This is income that can be generated from limited partnerships, joint venture investments, or real estate holdings.

It's not about working hard; it's about working smart. Focus on the things that will generate income. Delegate everything else!

SECOND, it's all about accumulating assets. Since the U.S. dollar was taken off the gold standard by Richard Nixon in 1971, I believe real value is in ASSETS—not dollars. In my opinion, real estate is the best asset your money can buy. I particularly like real estate because it can generate income (cash flow) and grow in value (equity appreciation). As you accumulate more assets you generate more income, in turn accumulating even more assets and in the process building wealth and legacy. Given the state of the current U.S. debt, high inflation is certainly in the future. We must hedge our investments against inflation. Cash flow with equity appreciation is the best way to do this.

The **THIRD** component to my freedom blueprint is mitigating the taxes. Realize that there are different ways to structure the way you receive income (both passive and active). Often simply by evaluating your business model and restructuring your corporate entities you can greatly reduce the effect of taxation.

I never truly understood the full impact taxes played in my ability to grow wealth until late in my career. This is a major key to financial freedom. Earned income is taxed at the highest tax bracket. Real estate assets provide not only the best wealth accumulation strategy but also one with the lowest possible tax.

The use of the self-directed Roth IRA is a strategy I share with you as a way to mitigate one of the biggest personal expenses: federal and state income taxes.

About all we have left that the IRS allows us to use without paying taxes along the way is a Roth IRA (Individual Retirement Account). Money certainly grows a whole lot faster if the IRS isn't taking its 25-40 percent share as fast as you make it. Every dollar the government takes is money that can't earn you a return. Unlike traditional IRA's, your contribution to the Roth IRA is made with after-tax dollars.

However, the money in the Roth IRA, including any earnings, can grow tax deferred and be withdrawn tax-free.

The information shared in this book is often contrary to conventional wisdom as taught by CPAs and financial planners. Consider yourself lucky if your CPA or attorney understands or is even aware that your IRA can be self-directed to buy real estate and other assets beyond the norm offered by banks and securities companies. Be careful from whom you take advice. At minimum, make certain whomever you're taking advice from is making more income than you!

There are specific IRS rules governing the different self-directed accounts. There are rules against what are known as prohibited transactions, such as "self-dealing" and "disqualified persons." You are prohibited from loaning money to or doing business with yourself or anyone in your linear descent or any entity you control.

There are also rules specific to IRAs as they relate to operating a business or buying houses with debt financing. The IRA is subject to pay taxes on the gain commonly referred to as UBIT (Unrelated Business Income Tax).

My goal is not for you to become an IRA expert but rather to use your IRA to earn and accumulate tax-free wealth. Once you've set up the IRA account with an approved third party administrator, they will walk you through the process and facilitate that first deal with you. It's that simple!

Your wealth will come from your ability to take a minimal amount of cash in your IRA (as little as $100) and use it to control real estate and other assets on which you can achieve a high rate of return. This is done by leveraging your knowledge and financial network of trusted advisors.

Remember, it's not the contribution that's important but what you use the IRA to buy and how much income that asset produces for the IRA.

As a comparison, let's assume we have $100,000 inside a Roth IRA and $100,000 outside it. We invest both at a 15% return, which can be easily done with minimal effort for a 10, 15, and 20 year term. The numbers below reflect the approximate values for this example.

	Taxed at 35%	Tax Free
10 years	$ 295,910	$ 437,195
15 years	$ 486,375	$ 920,185
20 years	$ 799,435	$1,937,935

Not using a Roth IRA would cost you over $1,000,000.

The above example assumes we did not add any more money to the principal. Now imagine what would happen if we add $100,000 dollars to the principal, each year for the first ten years. That number would be close to 2.5 million dollars. If we do nothing for ten more years except lend money out at 15%—the value jumps to 10.9 million dollars. The power of tax-free compounding!

There are many ways to structure deals using real estate inside your IRA. Let's use the example of a simple Option Contract. The IRA puts up an earnest money deposit on a Purchase & Sales Contract (an option). The IRA then assigns that contract to another investor to buy that property for a fee. The IRA puts out $100 dollars as earnest money and $1,000 dollars comes back to the IRA as an assignment fee.

Even a small amount inside an IRA can grow relatively quickly, and best of all, tax-free. Let's now take the same $1,000 from the option assignment and reinvest it in another deal. Now simply repeat the process.

You will soon realize that in order to have access to some of the best deals, you need access to deal makers and active real estate investors—people who do this for a living. More importantly, vetted real estate investors with a history of positive performance during periods of market volatility. Investors that uphold the core values of honesty, transparency, and integrity.

The following is an actual wholesale deal done inside a self-directed Roth IRA. The property consisted of a 1,000 square foot single family home needing a lot of repairs. The all-in price was $29,250 dollars (purchase price $25,000 with $4,250 in closing costs).

The market value of the property after repairs was estimated to be $180,000 dollars. The plan was for the Roth IRA to take title to this property. At the time, there was only about $5,000 dollars in the Roth IRA. We did have a traditional IRA with the needed funds for the purchase. However, we opted to do a partial conversion from the traditional to the Roth. We felt the anticipated ROI justified paying the tax on the $30,000 converted. We took out an additional $5,000 dollars to cover any carrying costs during the holding time.

The property was sold to a rehabber approximately six months later for $103,000 dollars. This property took longer to sell because the probate issues took longer than projected. Even with some of the legal expenses needed to clear title, there was over a 600% annual return on investment.

The purpose of this book is to awaken the financial genius inside YOU and make you aware of the tremendous opportunity in real estate. In this chapter, I focused on the Roth IRA as a vehicle to build your wealth tax-free. However, you don't need to become an expert in real estate investing to get involved.

The Key: surrounding yourself with a vetted network of trusted advisors and real estate investors, each bringing their own unique knowledge, experience, and resources to the real estate investing table.

Your goal is to align yourself with any of the coauthors/investors in this book and leverage their inner circle. You want to ride their coattails and piggyback on one of their deals. This is how you get started. This is how you learn. This is your fast track to financial freedom.

One thing is sure: people always need a place to live! Why not be in a business that fulfills the American Dream of home ownership? Why not work at something that produces income whether you are involved full-time or part-time? Why not be in a business that can make money in spite of the economy, interest rates, or the market situation. Best of all, why not be in a business that can produce income whether you're working or not.

You have the opportunity to take the future in your own hands. Your income and financial freedom is the result of one thing and one thing only: what you choose to do with your time! Remember it's not about working harder; it's about working smart!

It's also about the company you keep. Do not underestimate the influence others can have on the person you eventually become. The people around you matter.

Bottom line: the people you choose to spend time with or take advice from can have a profound effect on you personally and subsequently the success you achieve in life.

Enjoy the journey and appreciate every moment of life but choose wisely, and don't let others use your time unless you're willing to give it up.

ABOUT THE AUTHOR

GERRY J. CASAZZA graduated top of his class from Tufts University School of Dental Medicine in 1991.

Almost immediately after graduating, he started his own business, taking a small 700 square foot retail space and transforming it into a thriving dental practice, participating in every aspect of the design and construction process by doing 100% of the work himself. Talk about hands on! Gerry took on the carpentry, electrical, plumbing, and cabinetry all as a labor of love, but today he would be the first to tell you this is NOT the smartest approach. He has come to understand and appreciate the true value of one's time and the opportunities wasted on the often, unintentional squandering of time.

From the very beginning, Gerry took his calling as healer and oral physician very seriously, devoting thousands of continuing education hours to ongoing study and learning. For years, he traveled all over the United States seeking out the best mentors, clinicians, and educators in order to elevate his knowledge and skill set to better serve his patients.

As a testament to his growing success, he quickly outgrew his existing space.

Three years following the start-up, he purchased the commercial building he was in, and moved his office into the adjacent larger suite. For the second time, he undertook the process of expanding his office doing 100% of the work himself. Proving that habits and mindset are hard to break, and we often need to be reminded several times (if not more) before the lessons are learned.

In 2001, Gerry opened his second practice and felt as though he had arrived, seeing that he now needed to copy his diplomas for displaying in the second location.

By all accounts, he was very successful. He was also chained to the chair, bouncing between offices, working 12-14 hour days clinically, five to six days a week, and often on Sundays.

He was the self-appointed do-it-all person. Stress was high. Sleep a privilege. Family and personal time nonexistent. The proverbial "Golden Handcuffs."

It was not until October 2007 that Gerry's mindset regarding success and business changed forever. It was at a dental convention in Boston where he met a marketing guru by the name of Dan Kennedy. This was a life defining moment, changing not only the focus but also the direction of his life.

Gerry now challenges his previous mistaken views of life, success, money, happiness, and purpose. On that fateful day, Gerry was also introduced to a real estate guru who reignited his passion for real estate investing. This was the beginning of his entrepreneurial journey.

Today, Gerry leverages his dental degree by running a highly successful dental business, performing in the top 5% nationally. He works less than 16 hours per week clinically, not because he needs to but because he WANTS to! At any time, he could choose not to work at all because of the systems he's implemented so the business is no longer solely dependent on him. The extra time allows Gerry to explore entrepreneurial ventures including the opening of multiple dental offices as well as partnering in an active real estate investment business and real estate brokerage firm.

As a real estate investor, he deals primarily in his local market, but his lending and equity portfolio currently includes property in five states, and he continues to co-invest and joint venture in deals across the U.S.

Contact information:
gerrycasazza@gmail.com

W. Randall Cline

WORKING SMARTER, NOT HARDER

In 2014, I came across an email for dentists who were interested in pursuing real estate and saving on taxes. This caught my attention. I always had an interest in real estate, because most wealthy people in the world have made their money in real estate in some way. I looked further into the email and discovered Dr. David Phelps in Dallas, Texas. We spoke on the phone and he told me about a Mastermind group that he had started called Freedom Founders. It was by invitation only. After we spoke, he invited me to come as a guest to the next meeting to see if this was something that I was interested in. After this meeting, I was invited to join the group as a full member. I immediately felt that I had found a group with the same goals and vision that I had. I felt that Freedom Founders could help get me to where I wanted to be financially, without having to practice dentistry for the rest of my life. I was quite impressed with the program and network that Freedom Founders was made up of. I joined at the first meeting and I must say that it was probably the best decision I ever made. Always living within my means, I had saved money over the years, but this program gave me the potential to multiply my savings for retirement.

Before I joined Freedom Founders, my knowledge of real estate was limited to buying, selling, or renting residential or commercial property, of which I had personally done little or none. My first real estate deal happened in the fall of 2008. My son was in college and my wife and I decided to buy and restore an old house in this college town for my son and later on my daughter to use while in college. Instead of paying rather high rent for all those years, we wanted to own a house that would hopefully appreciate over the years and then sell later on for a profit. We purchased the house and then went about fixing it up. The house had been owned by an elderly couple who had not kept up with the routine maintenance of the house. The house needed a fair amount of work but it was mostly cosmetic repairs that were needed. We had no real budget or plan. About halfway through the project, we decided that we would sell the house instead of using it for the kids. Now this was in the fall of 2008 when the economy was in free fall. The repairs ended up costing more than expected, but then again we had no real experience at this. We finished the house after several months, listed it with a realtor, sold it, and made a $25,000 profit. What a miracle considering we were rookies at this game.

After my first meeting at Freedom Founders, I was amazed by the multiple aspects of real estate that I never knew existed. You don't know what you don't know. My head was spinning with all the different ways to get involved in real estate. I wanted to learn more to get clarity on all of this. However, as a dentist I thought that I had to completely understand it all before I could get involved. I thought that I had to be an expert before I could get involved. I was suffering from the typical paralysis of analysis that dentists usually have. Dr. Phelps told us that the most important action to take is to just get started and you can learn as you go. Freedom Founders has a cadre of trusted advisers from many different areas of real estate that will walk you through their area of expertise.

At my second meeting with Freedom Founders, I discovered that several members who joined about the same time as I did had already done a deal or two. I felt like I was behind already in my journey, so I told myself it was time to get started. With the help of David Phelps, I held my breath, took the plunge, and did my first real estate deal, as a short-term lender. By my third meeting three months later, I had done six more deals, and I was off and running. Each deal got easier and easier, and the process was becoming clearer. The fact of the matter is that there is enough hand holding during the process that David Phelps and the trusted advisers will keep you from making mistakes. Each trusted adviser has a system that they use for each and every deal. You do not have to reinvent the wheel. There are so many options for getting involved in real estate. You can be a lender, either short term (3-12 months) or longer term (1-5 years). You can buy and hold property for rentals and monthly cash flow or buy and sell individual performing or non-performing mortgage notes. You can buy into funds that buy and sell pools of mortgage notes. You can invest in funds that buy and hold multi-family units or funds that buy and hold trailer parks. The list goes on and on. I have tried to do some deals in all these different areas to test the waters to see which ones I like the best.

Before I go any further, I must say that much of what we have learned about real estate investing in Freedom Founders goes against the grain of conventional wisdom. Your typical financial advisers will tell you that real estate is very risky and you should limit your exposure to risk. They will say that being diversified in the stock market is the safest way to invest your money. Very few people know about or understand these investment tools. Financial advisers will not get involved in this type of investing because it is too sophisticated for the average investor. The establishment will not promote investing like this because they do not understand it and they cannot make a commission on it. This type of investing is really thinking outside of the box. In reality, it is much safer than investing in stocks and bonds, which I am convinced is manipulated and rigged against the average investor. The stock market is subject to every geopolitical or news event that occurs every day, subject to the latest catastrophe or the price of oil, and the list goes on and on. If you do your due diligence up front, you know which markets to get into and which ones to avoid, and you can limit your risk much better than in the stock market. I like having that type of control over my investments. Whenever a big news event occurs that rattles the stock market, nothing happens to the real estate deals that I have done. My lending deals still pay the same amount every month. My rentals still pay the same rent each and every month. The value of my owned properties does not change on a daily basis. My properties may not appreciate as much or my rents may not go up as much if something major happens to the economy, but my investment is still solid. However, investments in the stock market change daily.

I have done about forty short-term private lending deals in my two years of real estate investing using the Freedom Founders model. You can structure the deals any way you want with the borrower, without the bureaucracy of the banks and the time constraints. Most of these deals are done in a matter of 1-3 days in order to buy the properties at a discount. The deal must be a win-win for both parties and can be structured in a multitude of ways. If there are issues along the way, the deals can be modified between lender and borrower without a great deal of time or paperwork. There should always be a Plan B exit strategy built into the equation. No deal is perfect, and things can happen along the way, but you build that into the deal from the start.

These have all been deals involving single-family homes, specifically the three bedroom, two bath house. This is the basis for the Freedom Founders model. This size home is the typical American family home and makes up the vast majority of the residential real estate market. This size home will always be in demand unless something catastrophic happens to the economy. I like to work with homes not to exceed $140,000 in value because this is where you can get the most value out of the deal.

Another feature of the lending deals is that you have built in protection if the borrower defaults. The deal is structured so that the lender has not only a promissory note for repayment, but also gets a deed of trust for the property as security. The lender gets the property if the borrower defaults, and can either sell the property or hold and rent the property. There are no features like this in the stock market where your investment can go to zero.

In addition, I own rental units that provide a rental check each month, also known as mailbox money. Unlike dentistry, I get paid every month regardless of what I do or what the economy is doing. I am involved in three different funds similar to mutual funds where money is pooled together to buy multi-family apartment buildings. I am also involved in four long-term lending deals. Another great feature of these investments is that with the network of people I have established, you have access to buy, sell, or trade these deals with each other. I think I have just begun to scratch the surface of the limitless possibilities available in the real estate world. I have exceeded my dental income with passive income from real estate. I can now completely retire from dentistry, but I still enjoy doing it part-time without the pressure of having to do it for income.

My goal going forward is to teach my three grown children about this adventure. By starting at a much earlier age than me, time will work to their advantage, and they will have the opportunity to become financially free for life. What a great gift to give them and all who share the wisdom of this book.

ABOUT THE AUTHOR

My name is RANDY CLINE. I grew up in Kannapolis, North Carolina, about thirty miles from Charlotte, the largest city in the Carolinas. My next-door neighbor growing up was a family physician. His office was next door to his house, so I could always see his office and see how busy he was. It seemed that he worked all the time. I thought that I would like to become a physician, since the profession was so highly regarded at that time, and generally financially rewarding. I sought his advice about entering the profession, and he told me that if he had it to do over again, he would probably become a dentist because the hours were so much better and predictable. I explored the option of dental school and graduated from the University of North Carolina School of Dentistry at Chapel Hill in 1979. I started my own general dental practice from scratch in 1979. That is what most dental graduates did at that time. I visited several towns in North Carolina that were potential sites for a start-up practice, at the recommendation of a dental supply company. I decided upon Statesville, North Carolina, a town of about 30,000 people. I leased office space, set up the practice, and was off and running. I was young and eager to get to work and make my fortune.

After a year of practicing in this small town, I began thinking that there had to be more to practicing dentistry than I was experiencing. I was beginning to wonder if I had made the right career decision. I was not as busy as I wanted or needed to be to pay the bills. I answered an ad in the American Dental Association journal for a part-time associate in another small town about thirty miles away. The dentist had a large practice, and he was on the cutting edge of dental implants. Now this was in 1980, very early in the life cycle of implants before they were generally accepted in the profession. This dentist was quite a salesman, and I learned a great deal about dentistry and running a business. I worked with him for 1-2 days per week for about three years, and we decided to form a partnership after a short honeymoon of working together full time. I sold my original practice and joined him full time. Well, to make a long story short, the partnership never happened, and I left after another two years to go out on my own again.

I bought a well-established practice where I was the third-generation dentist in this practice. I grew the practice by a factor of four and then built a new facility. I practiced there for the next twenty-six years and was quite happy with the practice and life. Then the recession of 2007-2008 occurred, and business slowed down with the economy. I started looking for other options to increase my business, so I bought another practice in a town about fifteen miles away and became a multi-practice owner. In 2015, I sold my first practice, kept the second practice, and cut back to working two days per week, so I could pursue real estate as another source of income to help me create wealth. I hired associates to work in the practice with me. This was the first time I had worked with associates because I always thought I had to be in control, but it has all worked out better than I expected. I was learning how to delegate some of my responsibilities to give me the freedom to pursue my passion for real estate.

Contact information: randydds@windstream.net

Rajan Dhamrait

SEEING THE LIGHT

My work hard, trade "time for money", and invest in the stock market paradigm started to shift when I got involved with a dental/real estate mastermind called Freedom Founders. I was first introduced to Dr. Phelps and the Freedom Founders Mastermind two years ago. I purchased a DVD from Woody Oakes, a retired dentist and leading speaker in dentistry. This DVD showed Dr. Phelps talking about creating a financial plan B. The financial part of plan B is based on sound conservative real estate investing. I had done some investing in real estate in the past, but I was inspired by what Dr. Phelps had to say. Most of the material was new to me. I reached out to him and attended my first meeting two years ago. The benefits of this Mastermind extend well beyond the financial. I've become a part of a family. I network and have developed deep meaningful friendships with several fellow members.

As a real estate investor, I have a portfolio of numerous commercial and residential properties owned by various entities. Some of these entities include my self-directed IRA, Roth IRA, my children's Roth IRA, my children's ESA (Education Savings account), family HSA (Health Savings account), and numerous LLCs. I've owned some of this real estate for over twenty years. Over the years, I've spent countless hours and money studying and learning legal tax-saving strategies, asset protection, and proper legal structures. My portfolio has funded nine short-term hard money loans that involved investments, cumulatively exceeding one million dollars. Currently, my portfolio owns three commercial properties and seven residential properties. It has a significant investment in a mobile home fund that controls and owns hundreds of mobile home parks ... fifth largest in the U.S. The portfolio is one of the largest shareholders in four funds that control and own over 400 doors. Most of the properties in these four funds are upscale, and some of them are brand new construction. In the upcoming months, I will double or triple my real estate holdings. I've been delayed because it's been a tedious process to free up some of my retirement funds locked up in traditional pension plans. By no means am I trying to boast about the holdings of the portfolio. These investments reflect the knowledge, wisdom, and planning that has been done over the last two years since I've joined Freedom Founders. The extent of my real estate investing up to two years ago was two commercial properties and two residential properties. I've grown and learned by leaps and bounds since then.

I can't say I felt much anxiety getting started. That statement has some deep lying undertones. I wasn't anxious because of the openness, experience, support, integrity, accountability, and credibility of the individuals involved with Freedom Founders, especially the trusted advisers. They've been through the ups and downs. They've been through the meltdowns in the real estate world. A deal looks good on paper, but the real learning comes from mistakes, or learning opportunities as it is commonly phrased. The trusted advisers and the rest of our group are very open and candid about discussing mistakes. We've overcome the barrier that holds most people back. Most of us hesitate to discuss our mistakes because of our ego and flat out not wanting to admit we made a mistake. We set aside all egos when we walk into Freedom Founders and learn and share with others.

One of the components of overcoming anxiety, having peace of mind with real estate, and the ability to step out of the box is accountability. There is a high level of accountability within Freedom Founders. To start with, we rely on the trusted advisers for opportunities, and they rely on us. This trickles down the entire food chain. The property manager is much more responsive to the trusted adviser who helped us purchase the property because they know the adviser has many more clients. A plumber is more likely to respond to the property manager's service requests knowing that that property manager manages 500 doors for members of our group.

Another component of the ability to step out of the box is based on integrity. It's been exciting to have some of my hard money loan deals bring back good returns ... well above stock market returns in a safer, more predictable environment. However, sometimes things don't go smoothly, and integrity becomes even more important. I made the promised return on my first large private lending deal even though the borrower lost money on the deal. He values his relationship with Freedom Founders and wanted to maintain his integrity. This would be less likely to happen if you are going it alone.

Like many, I do suffer from paralysis by analysis. I have the double whammy. I have an engineering degree ... I tend to be uptight and very analytical ... show me the data and evidence! To compound that, most of us dentists want everything to be perfect 100% of the time. As much as we don't want to admit it, we have attitudes that reflect our academic success. Most of us excelled academically. In high school, I was an Illinois State scholar, and I received sizable scholarships and awards in both engineering school and dental school. It's important to remember that expertise in one arena doesn't make you an expert in all arenas. To paraphrase a famous quote "You don't learn if you're the smartest individual in the room." There are numerous experts involved with the group. We have experts in estate planning, real estate notes, multifamily and single family housing, wholesaling, rent to owns, rehabbing, leadership skills, virtual assistants, real estate law, marketing, business growth and development, etc. Being a part of the Freedom Founders mastermind is like having an objective board of directors, a success team, a peer advisory group, a board of experts, and accountability partners, all rolled into one. Cumulatively, this helps me overcome some of my paralysis by analysis ... including writing this chapter.

I followed the typical path of success ... work hard, make sacrifices, and pursue education. This is even more reinforced in the Asian Indian community. Like many professionals, I made many sacrifices for my practice. I spent countless hours that extended into the evenings and weekends. Like many others, I had tendencies to get settled in with my live and get tunnel vision. I traded time for dollars. I would do it all over again the same way based on what I knew at that time. I followed the typical pathway to financial security. Work hard, be conservative in your spending, save as much as you can, and invest in the stock market. I used respected well-intentioned financial advisers. But the results were mediocre. Most of us, including myself, experienced years where the advisers made money even though we lost money ... sometimes sizable chunks. I worried about my financial security. As an Asian American, I embrace the obligation to pay for my children's college education, including graduate school (MD, DDS, JD, PhD). This compounds the financial security stress. I, like many others, have felt the anxiety created by the ups and downs of the market. I invested in the Enron's and WorldCom's and have lost everything. Yet, I continued on the same path, hoping and praying. The Freedom Founders mastermind has changed my mindset and brought me peace.

Most of us successful professionals have had to go it alone. We've had to go through our own trials and errors. My involvement in the Freedom Founders mastermind has greatly accelerated my learning curve with real estate investing by not having to go it alone and learning from a group of wonderful people who truly and unselfishly want you to be successful. I feel like I've cheated my way to years of experience ... I feel like I've received the CliffsNotes. We are constantly learning and improving. We spend countless hours devoted to podcasts, books, lectures, other masterminds, networking, etc. We keep up with current trends. The hours and dedication that are put in cumulatively could never be accomplished by one person. This is even more difficult when one is still running a busy dental practice and is heavily involved with the family. I can't overstate the unselfish component of this mastermind. Collectively the group, Dr. Phelps, and the trusted advisers have decades and decades of experiences and serve as a secondary conscience. I'm excited about the road ahead. Just like life I know I will face challenges in the real estate arena. But, it's refreshing to know I'm not going down the path alone. I can see the light at the end of the tunnel, and I know I can back off trading time for dollars.

ABOUT THE AUTHOR

RAJAN "RAJ" DHAMRAIT has practiced general dentistry in central Illinois for over twenty-seven years. With the help of a scholarship, he attended the University of Iowa College of Dentistry and graduated in 1989. Raj started his dental career by operating a small dental practice in rural Illinois and working as an associate in Bloomington and Springfield, Illinois, for seven years. In 1996, he purchased a large existing practice in Springfield, Illinois. The practice has enjoyed much success, mainly due to Raj's dedication, hard work, and hours of continuing education ... the forever student. In essence, his life's focus has been on dentistry and serving the needs of others. He was fortunate to identify his path in life early. Many people struggle with this and spend several years pursuing other paths. From his recollection, he aspired to be a dentist about the age of twelve. He feels blessed and honored to be a part of this noble profession. He's grateful for the support of so many people and organizations over the years—most notably his parents.

Like most individuals, his background, and his parents, plays an integral part of his mindset throughout his life. He's first generation Asian American. His parents are from India, and his father earned a Masters Degree in Civil Engineering in the U.S. in the fifties, which was rather rare. He grew up in a loving, structured, and conservative environment, driven somewhat by his father's engineering mindset. He was born and raised in Illinois. Except for his years at the University of Iowa, he has lived in Illinois his entire life, living most of early life as a minority. He grew up in an era when American-born Asian Indians were a very small minority in rural Illinois. He and his sister were the first Asian Indians to attend their high school of two thousand students. He was one of the few American born Asian Indians at the University of Iowa (28,000 students) in the early 1980s. Even though his parents are Indian immigrants, he grew up with the American culture, partly due to his father coming to the U.S. at a young age, but mainly because he had little exposure to the Indian culture in small town Illinois. His parents realized that to live and succeed in the United States you have to embrace the American culture to some point.

Even though he had little exposure to the Indian culture, he was immersed in the Asian Indian and immigrant mindset. That mindset was, and still is, to place a heavy emphasis on their children. The most important thing is a college education, especially at the graduate degree (MD, DDS, PhD, JD) level. They're even more worried about financial and family security because they're immigrants and have nothing to fall back on. They believe in hard work and sacrifice. With this mindset, it was difficult for Dr. Raj to take his nose off the grindstone and learn to work smarter instead of harder.

Dr. Raj skipped his senior year of high school and started college early. He received a degree in Biomedical Engineering from the University of Iowa in 1985. Even though he had a desire to be a dentist from an early age, he pursued engineering as an undergraduate. In line with his parents' and his mindset, his college plan B, or security net, was engineering. In case he didn't get accepted into dental school, he would still have a viable and respectful career as an engineer. He's always lived his life trying to have a backup plan.

Dr. Raj has been involved in numerous civic, professional, and education-related organizations over the years. He served as a delegate to the Illinois State Dental Society for seven years. He's been the legislative chair for the GV Black Dental Society for over seven years. He's been on numerous boards of organizations and served as president of the local Rotary Club in the early 1990s. His passion is helping others. He's looking forward to playing an integral role in organizing and hosting the Mission of Mercy (MOM) event in Springfield, Illinois, in 2018. The goal of MOM is to treat under-served patients with serious dental needs. In 2016, eight hundred volunteer dentists, hygienists, assistants, dental students, lab technicians, pharmacists, and lay volunteers treated nearly 1300 children and adults during a two-day period in Collinsville, Illinois. Over $1.1 million in much needed dental care was provided. Dr. Raj has volunteered as a dentist in two previous MOM events.

Dr. Raj has been married for twenty years and is proud of his seventeen-year-old daughter and fourteen-year-old son.

Contact information:
rajbo@aol.com

Jonathan and Rose Gillesby

MENTORSHIP IS THE KEY

We are not very exciting people. We are not overly creative, daring, or adventurous. We have been the play it safe couple our entire lives. While for the most part it has served us well, there comes a time when you need to take the blinders off, look up from what you are doing, and ask yourself if this path you are on is really taking you where you want to go?

Our blinders came off in 2015.

Despite our very predictable life, there was one way we were different, and I shouldn't say 'we.' It was really Jon. Maybe not so different than you, as you are reading this book. It started because for years Jon was restless regarding our investments. He knew we had good incomes, yet he was not satisfied with what we spent, how we spent it, how we saved it, and how it was invested. He knew there had to be a way for the money we were saving to work harder for us. Like you, we were working very hard and wanted our savings to do the same. We were, and continue to be, an extremely busy family. Thankfully, it was in careers that motivated and interested us, but it was still stressful and took us away from each other and our kids for much more than the 40 hours a week for which we had hoped.

Jon has always focused on educating himself. If he has an interest in something, he jumps in with both feet to understand all he can about it. He has logged countless hours of continuing education in order to bring more advanced dental procedures to the small community he serves with his practice. Hours consumed by continuing education of course means hours spent away from the family. Between Rose's career and consulting work she traveled a lot as well, which added to the craziness. The boys were growing fast and college was looming in the not-so-distant future. What would be the best way to fund college and our eventual retirement? Why not follow the masses? If everyone is investing in the stock market it must be the best way to reach your financial goals, right?

So, we tried things. Jon is a researcher at heart, so he dove into every book, seminar, and meeting he could find. He learned a ton. The stock market was no longer just a crap shoot. We dabbled in e-commerce and real estate. It wasn't long before we realized real estate was actually interesting to both of us, but we didn't know what we were doing. To complicate things: like many wives, Rose is risk averse. She prefers the safe route. Getting the boys through college was all she really cared about and didn't look much beyond that. The stock market was a known entity. It was what everyone else was doing and she felt like we were doing the right thing by piling money into our 401K's and the stock market. Although she couldn't deny this wasn't getting us very far very fast. Even with a small library of financial education books to help us, we were only beating the market averages by a small margin. And what if the ever-increasing market volatility is the new norm? Better hope the market doesn't reset once you've reached your number like we saw happen to family and friends in 2008.

Up until April of 2015, our investment knowledge base had been self-educated and pieced together with us working to beat the stock market. Our coffee table and book shelves were littered with the likes of Robert Kiyosaki, James Bogle, and Burton Malkiel, as well as

Money and *Kiplinger's* magazines. We also kept tabs on the latest real estate trends. Always intriguing, but mainly consisting of some television infomercials on how to flip foreclosures. We invested in a small wheelbarrow full of books and CDs that would turn us into experts. Thank goodness after researching we decided not to cut our teeth on real estate at that time—it happened to be 2007. Without access to experienced advisors/mentors who understand how to invest whether the cycle is up or down, we would have most assuredly been another casualty to the real estate crash. We spent a lot of time and money developing a long term financial plan with a well-respected financial planner as well as learning and applying a debt reduction system. Both were good things. Both expanded our financial education. However, neither were getting us where we wanted to go. After fifteen years of really trying to understand the best methods of investing we had just over a 4% annualized rate of return. Our accounts continued to grow, giving us the feeling that we were successful investors. But the truth was we were really only successful savers.

In April of 2015, while I sat looking through the emails I hadn't gotten to during my normal crazy week, I found an advertisement from a dentist touting financial freedom. Why I even spent more than the time it takes to delete an email, I will never know, but it was 30 seconds that would change the path my family was taking. David Phelps spoke of how we could leave a world of working hard for our money and enter the world of having our money work for us. It was a door we were a little concerned about walking through (Rose was terrified), but we are both so thankful we did.

In reading David's story, I could relate to him. We were similar people. It was that recognition of our common thoughts and goals that led me to reach out to him. I have always enjoyed reading others success stories and gleaning knowledge from them, but our similarities made David's story seem possible for us. I could envision myself doing the things he talked about. It was exciting!

Our past experience in purchasing real estate had left us with one property that we still own today due to a lack of multiple exit strategies and little to no due diligence prior to making the purchase. We bought in a bubble market with the plan to build a home on that property. When life took us in a different direction—no exit strategy existed. Despite a disappointing experience, real estate continued to intrigue us, but we lacked access to a true mentor and a network of real estate professionals and financial friends (lenders, brokers, wholesalers, self-directed IRA custodians, accountants, flippers, etc.). This is what David taught us. The importance of the relationships. The importance of our network. We know today that our network is our net worth.

David gave us access to some of the most successful, knowledgeable, honest, and accomplished real estate professionals in almost every individual niche of real estate. We have built relationships with these people. Jumped on planes, drove long hours to see their businesses and gotten to know them and their teams. While we value all the knowledge gained from these great people and their individual niches, we have come to determine our own path in real estate lies within a combination of rental property acquisition, investment in real estate fund projects, and lending to other investors.

Once we determined the right niche of real estate for our particular life stage and goals, it was time to begin looking for our first deal. We soon realized there was some much needed preparation, so we dove into learning about self-directed IRA's and the benefits of not only having one, but really putting the money in an IRA to work. We spent the travel time coming home from our first meeting, getting account balances, determining funds that could be transferred, and determining the amount of capital we had available to begin investing. In no time at all, one of our new financial friends had us set up with a self directed IRA and were teaching us how to invest it. Next, we reached out to a few turnkey rental providers we had been introduced to and just like that…we were buying a house in Tennessee. Wow! We were nervous, but we had done our homework, we knew this real estate strategy made so much more sense for our financial future that we had to find the courage to jump in and make this deal.

Within the first fifteen months that first rental property turned to three, then seven, then sixteen—and now we have a rapidly expanding portfolio with properties in five states generating significant monthly cash flow. In addition, we have invested in other types of real estate (mobile home parks, apartment complexes, condominiums funds) in many other states. We have also taken the position as the lender in various other deals. All of these investments are earning returns that are greater (by multiples) than what we have achieved in the stock market.

We have discovered that there is quite a range of what can be considered passive real estate investing. Acquiring properties to become rentals is the most time intensive. The process of researching the property, obtaining financing, purchasing, possible rehabbing, and managing the property management companies can become a part time job if you wish to be aggressive in building a portfolio. As would be expected, if you have built a good network of people to help you do this wisely, the returns are generally the highest. For those looking to have a more truly passive investment, finding someone with whom to partner or joint venture is the key. By taking the role of the lender position in a real estate transaction (with someone you know, like, and trust) you can earn a good return, while having that loan secured by a piece of real estate. (Wall Street never offered us this kind of insurance plan on our investments.)

This route has the added bonus of being simple, or requiring less "brain damage" as an investor friend of ours likes to put it. You don't have to build the network, work on the relationships, attend conferences, or learn the business of real estate. You can just invest—and while you may not earn quite the returns of a more hands on real estate investor, you can easily earn returns that exceed volatile stock market performance. Those returns can go right back into another deal—keeping your money working for you. This type of win-win collaboration with private investors has become the most satisfying investments for us to date. Solid single-family real estate in stable areas that is purchased at wholesale prices, allowing joint ventures with private lenders to reap mutually satisfying returns. We can help others turn their stagnant savings into healthy returns! With the knowledge we have gained over the last eighteen months, we have often found ourselves just shaking our heads with how much time and effort (not to mention angst and worry) we spent spinning our wheels in the stock market for much lower (and unsecured) returns.

The co-contributors to this book have reached a common conclusion: real estate investing in its many facets either is, or soon will be, the vehicle that provides lifestyle freedom and the ability to focus on passions and helping others, while having the security that we will be financially secure.

ABOUT THE AUTHORS

In all honesty, Jon and Rose Gilles-by are very ... typical, for lack of a better adjective. With goals and aspirations that are probably very similar to yours, given you are reading this book. We were blessed to have hard-working and supportive parents who had high expectations. Subsequently, we have been hard workers since grade school (which is where we met by the way). We kept our noses down and got the grades. We earned our degrees (Rose is a veterinarian and Jon a dentist) and were ready to take on the real world. We were fortunate to settle back into our home town, where both our families and many friends live and were around for support. All parents know there is nothing like having those go-to grandparent babysitters nearby!

After a couple years, Jon became a partner at a successful dental office and Rose made a transition from mixed animal small town vet, to a career in the pharmaceutical industry. We have been very fortunate to have careers that challenge us and allow us to provide well for ourselves and our two sons. With a family comes the responsibility to start saving and investing what you can to provide for retirement and college educations (if you chose to do so). We (okay, Jon) have always had an interest in how to get the most out of those hard-earned dollars that we saved for the future.

Jon loves to learn and took on the task of learning how to invest. That is where the trouble lies though. There are so many experts that have different ideas on why, where, and how to invest for the most success. Investing in the stock market seemingly provided the most options, and it was what everyone else was doing. It took longer than we care to admit to learn that if everyone is doing it, we should be looking for another path. Again, that took a long time to sink in (until August 2015 to be precise) so Jon spent much of his time trying to learn from the stories of successful stock investors and apply that to their savings.

Making a long story short, earning basically market average on our own led us to develop a plan with a well-respected independent financial advisor. The number they laid in front of us as the necessary nest egg to maintain our lifestyle in retirement was like a punch in the gut. Given our age and propensity for saving it would be doable. It just wasn't going to be doable to become job optional earlier than reaching our sixties. That is a goal of ours—to become financially free as soon as possible. Not because we don't want a job, but because we don't want to rely on a job. We have very little faith in the path our elected officials have been taking our country down for some time, and only fear it may get worse. Financial freedom gives us more opportunities to provide significance and be able to enjoy whatever work we do as a want to, rather than a need to. So, we found ways to save more and reduce debt more quickly. We slowly worked at moving the date to reach our number closer.

Real estate investing had always been appealing, especially as we discovered Robert Kiyosaki and some of his published works. We would get excited about a possible opportunity but not act due to a lack of real understanding and fear. "Paralysis by analysis" is the more accurate description (it used to be one Jon's specialties). If we only had someone who we could work with that had been down the path before us and was willing to share their knowledge.

For us, that opportunity came when we met former practicing dentist, David Phelps. David had accomplished exactly the things we strived for financially, using real estate as the vehicle. He has chosen a path of significance that provides education and mentorship to others interested in taking control of their financial futures. Jon now has a new passion to dive head long into and learn from an amazing group of successful investors. The difference of having a personal connection and a network with whom you invest is monumental. Working with people that you know, like, and trust is the ultimate advantage.

Jon was even able to shed that analysis paralysis and our investment future has been on a very different path since. Now, we're not going to fill a page with lots of flowery words about how much time we have, how little stress we have, and no longer need our jobs. None of that is true for us yet, but we now know that it will happen. Continuing on our new path will give us the freedom to choose how we spend our time… and it's not far off. Enjoy reading the stories some of our friends have been gracious enough to share in their individual chapters. It is not only about why real estate, but a collection of the financial journeys of high achieving professionals whom either have already achieved, or soon will, that freedom so many of us desire. We hope that they give you the push to take control of your own financial future and join us on the journey!

Enjoy this book. If nothing else, we hope it makes you think.

Best,
Jon and Rose Gillesby

Contact information:
gillesbyj@gmail.com
Cell: (269) 655-5999m

John Harasin

THE CARROT AND THE STICK

The shift in momentum is discussed in sports all the time. It is the same in achieving your goals; you need that drive. Once you are on a roll, you have to keep it going. What is your carrot? What is your stick? Have they changed over your lifetime? I bet they have. What do you fear? Why is this important? Because you need your carrots and sticks to overcome your fears and step out of your comfort zone. You own all four of these; they are different and personal for each one of us. Further, you must realize that a goal without a plan and action is nothing more than a dream. You need a big enough WHY to motivate yourself to take action, overcome your fears, move ahead with your plan, and maintain momentum.

In the book *The Compound Effect* by Darren Hardy, the author talks about the tremendous value of doing a little each day toward your goals. As an example, in order to keep my momentum going, I read at least ten pages of a nonfiction book each day. That adds up to 3,650 pages a year. I highly recommend doing this; get audio books for your commute as well. List areas of your life you would like to change or improve and chunk it down into bite-sized pieces as described in the book, *The Slight Edge* by Jeff Olson. Let me show you how this approach has changed my life.

Like you, I get a lot of email. Why I opened one named *Freedom Founders*, I have no idea. The title might suggest I was a prepper looking for a doomsday group to join. No, I was looking for freedom from the hamster wheel I was on. That day, David Phelps (CEO of Freedom Founders), standing in front of his bookcase in his office, spoke to me. Freedom Founders is a mastermind community that helps healthcare professionals develop a customized freedom blueprint. The blueprint consists of where you are and where you want and need to be, now and in the future. It involves practice building skills through the use of sound business principles and building your net worth using real estate as the vehicle.

The goals are simple to understand and adaptable to each individual. First, develop a business that is sustainable and has systems in place so it can prosper even if the doctor/owner is not there. Second, create a diversified portfolio of real estate investments whose profits will fund your desired lifestyle. Needless to say, this peaked my curiosity. I had a big enough WHY, overcame my fear, acted and went to my first meeting in Dallas.

This wasn't my first rodeo. My entire career, I had been in search of multiple streams of income (a satellite office, multilevel marketing programs multiple times). I had attended a real estate for dentists course, which led me on a journey of learning in which I spent $100,000 in continuing education and travel. That only led to another $100,000 loss in a commercial real estate deal gone bad during the collapse in 2010. My carrot, at that time, was the lake house my wife and I dreamed about, and the stick was the freedom of having to make that number every month in my dental practice.

As a result of past experiences, I entered that first Freedom Founders meeting with a healthy amount of skepticism. When I left, I knew I was in the right room with the right people because everybody was much smarter than me. I am very competitive, and I felt the need to learn and understand what these other people knew (carrot and stick #2.) As a point of enlightenment, I have learned you don't need to know it all before taking action; knowledge comes with time, action expedites the process.

My skepticism was further lifted because the principle of real estate just made sense. The stock market has never made sense to me. No one could ever answer my questions to my satisfaction. How are you supposed to live off your returns and never touch your principle, much less have your principle grow to compensate for inflation in a down market? In a down market, you have eroded your principle by your withdrawals, your losses, and inflation. Not to mention, the never-ending fees.

Sensible real estate investing means using homes everyone needs as a hard asset to propel your wealth building. Ideal is a three bedroom, two bath house with a two-car garage with a value (depending on the location) under $150K. Why? Rent is affordable, and it cash flows. In addition, one needs to realize what happens when the real estate market goes down—nothing. Have you ever heard of rent going down?

Your asset may be worth less, but it still cash flows the same. And when the real estate market rebounds, your asset regains its value. The key take away, in an up or down market, the checks keep coming. People still need a roof over their heads. When the market is down, it is the time to buy; and when the market is up, it is your choice to sell your asset and take the profit. Unlike the stock market, this is truly a beautiful thing!

When we returned from our first meeting, we had written an action plan, but in all honesty, we were overwhelmed from information overload. At the same time, we knew we had specific tasks to accomplish to be accountable to the group. Yes, another stick. We began listening to CDs and reading about investing in real estate. We also opened two self-directed IRAs. Baby steps, but hearing and reading the concepts and principles we had heard in our first meeting led to greater understanding and clarity.

At our second meeting, one of my fellow members won an award for what he and his son had accomplished. Stick and carrot, I wanted that award. In the next three weeks, I did what I was told to do, and well, maybe a little in excess. I visited trusted advisors in three different states, invested in all three businesses, eight deals in total, invested in three funds, rolled my 401(k) into a self-directed IRA, and we were off and running and haven't stopped yet. By the way, at the next meeting, I won the *Massive Action* award! Action taken, carrots and sticks used, fears overcome, goal accomplished!

In all sincerity, you don't have to jump in with both feet. As I met personally with the trusted advisors and their teams, I witnessed their organizations and integrity, and knew this was the right thing for me. For those who may not share my passion, you can still accomplish your goals by joint venturing with others and learning as you go. There is no magic here; you must take action to move forward. Start by finding your why. If you need help, read *Start With Why* by Simon Sinek. Part of your why are your personal carrots and sticks that will drive you to take action and create and maintain momentum.

Sustained, continued growth leads to the compound effect. Even if the growth is small, it will have considerable impact. The stories in this book are living proof this is possible no matter where you are in life. Today, after two and a half years of investing in real estate, my wife and

I are personally and financially free. Your time frame may be different, but it will never happen if you don't start. Someday is a day that never happens. Make today your someday so you can begin the first chapter of your book *Financial Freedom by Investing in Main Street, Not Wall Street*.

ABOUT THE AUTHOR

JOHN HARASIN is a competitor and a survivor. You want him on your team because he refuses to give up. He started his young adult life being told by a high school counselor that he was not college material. The counselor made this assumption based on a 50% score in reading comprehension on his SAT. He felt John would be better off seeking a career working in the local Ford Motor plant. That lit a competitive fire! The counselor overlooked his 98% score in mathematics. John applied to engineering schools, and went on to attend The University of Michigan.

He struggled his freshman year, taking eighteen credits a term and had mediocre grades. He worked hard his next three years to raise his grade point average, and he was accepted into The University of Michigan School of Dentistry. To his chagrin, in June he received a letter informing him that a law referred to as "affirmative action" had been passed. His position had been given to another student, and he would have to reapply the next year. John and his microbiology lab partner (who had received a similar letter from the medical school) went into panic mode looking for a solution to this dilemma. They found a masters program in cell chemistry that had openings. They read everything that the department head had ever written, interviewed, and were both accepted into the program. John needed 36 credit hours to complete the master's program. Not seeing the light of day for eight months, he received his masters and was on to dental school.

Dental school, for John and his classmates, was a boot camp, possibly to get them ready for the rigors of private dental practice. Regardless, it was a four-year test of sheer willpower. Unfortunately, there is nothing taught about life after dental school. No counseling on options for employment or mentorships. No classes taught on the business of dentistry, much less financial planning for future retirement. The thought at the time was to get an associateship, buy into the practice, and eventually sell the practice to fund your retirement. Not a very sound plan, if a plan at all. During the first ten years of his dental career, he and his wife (a dental hygienist) made a good living. They managed to buy their first house (interest rates were 17%), buy a practice, build a new office building, build the house that they live in to this day, and build what they thought was a substantial nest egg. Life was moving along smoothly.

Then, the day of awakening occurred! John's parents lived a mile from his office and were having lunch with him one day. They had received a free copy of Money Magazine. The featured article discussed the amount of savings required in order to retire. It took into account your current age, your desired retirement age, your desired income at retirement, inflation, and interest earned on investments. John wished he had kept that magazine. At the time, he was thirty-seven years old. His goal was to replace his current income, and he had saved what he considered a substantial amount towards that goal between his IRAs, brokerage accounts, savings, etc. As he tabulated the number he would need to retire at his target age of 55, he choked on his sandwich. He was only 10% of his way there. That started the wheels turning. He needed to kick it up a notch. Thinking back to that day, John wondered what would have happened if he had not picked up that magazine. When would he have woken up to reality, or would he be like 95% of people today who cannot retire at 65 years of age at the same lifestyle they had during their years practicing? Today, there is more information available about retirement needs, yet the average age of retirement for a dentist has increased to age 68. To protect the innocent, names will not be mentioned along John's bumpy road to prosperity.

The Michigan Dental Association endorsed the first company he went to. They did an economic freedom analysis, and set up a savings and investment plan based on what they termed a conservative 13% return. During his time with this group, the return never reached 6%, much less the 13% they promised. While at a continuing education course in Atlanta, John was having dinner with a couple of fellow dentists. From their conversation, it was obvious to him that they were doing quite well with their investment advisor. He got the advisor's name and paid the $10,000 fee to have another economic freedom analysis. This company was very thorough. Their projections were made on an 8% return, much more conservative and realistic than the previous analysis. That being said, under their watch, he did well until 2008-2010 when the company failed to get out of the market and lost a third of John's accumulated savings. In 2013, the market was shaky, and trying to avoid another loss, John pulled all of his money out of the market. While the money sat idle in cash, he noticed he was being charged $2800 a month in fees. The old saying never rang truer; "nobody cares about your money as much as you do." It was time for John to take charge of his own money and how it was invested.

During this twenty year process, John had dragged his wife into several multilevel marketing programs, and a real estate for dentists program that led to a $100,000 loss in a commercial real estate deal that went south during the 2008-2010 real estate crash. He was always looking for multiple sources of income to no avail. Money Magazine was John's first "ah ha" moment; his second came in an email. He went to the well one more time and feels his wife deserves sainthood for this. He said, "Jeannie, we are going to Dallas." What David Phelps, the CEO of Freedom Founders, said in an email spoke directly to him. Persistence, fortitude, and the drive to never give up finally paid off. Today, he and his wife are personally and financially free.

Life is not a straight or smooth road. You have to adjust to the turns and bumps along the way. Don't let anyone tell you what you can or cannot accomplish in life. This is your life to live, and take pride in proving them wrong. Use this as motivation to never, ever give up. Freedom is just around the next corner. This book is a composite of stories from different members of the Freedom Founders mastermind. They are all at different levels on their journey to financial freedom. John's mission is to pass this message on to others so that they can see the power of sensible investment in real estate as an asset class. His hope is that this book will be your Money Magazine and open your eyes to a road to financial freedom.

Contact information:
jmharasin@gmail

David Phelps

A MOMENT OF TRUTH

This was never part of the orignal plan…

I had laid out my entire life in advance. "I've got this—the sky's the limit." Blessed with good intellect and a work ethic to boot. Failure was not an option. A perfect family. A perfect life. A perfect professional practice career.

But there I was. Sitting on the small, vinyl, padded bench in Jenna's hospital room. The IV machine humming, holding several bags of fluids and meds, dripping into the tubes that ran into her small and bruised hand, the needles carefully taped against her skin to hold them stable.

Jenna, only twelve years old, is asleep; her body still trying to recover from an exhaustive six hours of surgery removing her cirrhotic and failed liver and replacing it with the gift of life—a donor's liver.

Away from my busy and stressful practice, I had a lot of time to think at that hospital.

No cell phone access. Disconnected from the rest of the world, nothing else mattered. All of the daily "stuff" that had seemed so paramount wasn't even a blip on my radar.

All of my education, wisdom, and experience; even all of the money I could earn—none of it mattered. None of it could make a difference.

I could only hope.

Hope and pray that Jenna would recover and I would get a second chance. A second chance to be a father—a real father who would be present, not absent. Not preoccupied with "stuff."

Would there be a "someday?" A day in the future when I could spend quality time with Jenna?

Time is never on our side. It marches on. There is a limited supply for each one of us. Tomorrow is not promised to anyone. Life is a gift.

It was during Jenna's initial weeks of transplant recovery while spending day after day at Texas Children's Hospital in Houston, that I made a critical and life-changing decision.

A moment of truth.

I would no longer practice dentistry.

Creating a Plan B. While a senior in college, I began reading books about investments (I always had a knack for planning ahead). I read books about stock market investing and some about real estate. Comparing the two, real estate won hands down. It was a tangible asset that I could control.

Investing in the stock market made no sense to me.

During my first year of dental school at Baylor College of Dentistry in Dallas (1980), I talked my dad into being my co-venture partner in acquiring a two-story brick rental house (an estate sale) in a solid Dallas neighborhood. We followed the fundamental rule of real estate; buy the worst house in a good neighborhood.

I learned how to manage this first asset for rental income. After graduation from Baylor in 1983, we sold the house and split about $50,000.00 in capital gain profit (capital gains are taxed at a much lower rate than ordinary, or active income).

The epiphany for me was in realizing that I made a capital profit of $25,000.00 from this one real estate asset during the same period of time that I worked many, many hours as a waiter at night and on weekends with much less to show in net income.

Why should I work for money all of my life when I could acquire good capital assets that would work for me whether I worked or not?

I began to understand that if I could acquire enough assets, I wouldn't have to work as hard...maybe not at all.

By continuing to purchase and invest in real estate, I was transitioning from working for money to investing money in capital assets that would produce cash flow, preserve and build wealth. This was my "Plan B."

Creating a Plan B was the key to my financial freedom. It was there when I needed it/wanted it.

In 2004, with Jenna in the hospital, I decided to pull the trigger.

Hard work, sacrifice and a disciplined approach to real estate investment, provided the foundation that allowed me to give up my good, but very restrictive career as a dentist.

Not an easy decision, but I had a real "reason why."

Update on Jenna. Today, she is in college working towards an associates degree in occupational therapy. A published author, speaker... she's got the world by the short hairs. Pretty good for a kid who, at age sixteen, was reading and writing at a second-grade level (She suffered through intense chemotherapy as a very young child to fight high-risk leukemia and suffered epileptic seizures from age eight to twelve). She missed the first thirteen years of a "normal" kid's life.

Courageous, driven, tenacious, a fighter. My girl.

Here's what I learned...

Network or connections are the most important factor in orchestrating a secure financial future. It is also the most underutilized capital asset. Who you know is essential. Creating relationships is the hardest part of making real estate a viable investment and also the reason why so many novice investors fail. They try to do it all themselves.

It takes time and work to establish these critical relationships. Many underestimate this crucial piece!

Why do you do what you do?

"David," other dentists ask me, "why aren't you retired?"

What they mean is, "If you did so well with real estate and dentistry, why are you still going at it?"

Fair question.

It's true that I don't need to do…anything, really.

For me, I do what I do because it's the most significant way I can invest my time.

A genuine passion for helping my colleagues break the chains from being slaves to their practices, their financial fears and helping them create freedom in their lives and the lives of their families, this passion demands my attention.

I love the fact that this gives me a platform and brings some of the best and brightest people in all areas of business, marketing, real estate, and finance, to Dallas four times a year.

This community is my best insurance policy. With the volatility and unknowns in our economy and industry, bringing together a Board of Advisors allows us to stand apart from the fallout and find the opportunities that chaos brings.

Being in the middle of all of the real estate opportunities within our group allows me to put deals together and help our members use various buckets of investment capital in the safest, most efficient, effective means possible.

Having the freedom to retire, and actually doing it, are worlds apart for me. I'll likely never retire in the typical sense. Remaining significant and relevant until my body and mind gives out, now that sounds like a plan!

My community and relationships gives me the platform to do just that.

What a gift!

ABOUT THE AUTHOR

David Phelps, D.D.S

Founder & CEO, Freedom Founders Mastermind

David Phelps owned and managed a private practice dental office for over twenty-one years. While still in dental school in 1980, he began his investment in real estate by joint-venturing with his father on his first rental property. Three years later, the property was sold and David took his $25,000 capital gain share and leveraged it into thirty-one properties that produced $15,000 monthly net cash flow by 1998.

Multiple health crises suffered by his daughter, Jenna (leukemia, epilepsy and a liver transplant at age 12), compelled David to leave private practice to be there for his daughter. Today, with a true freedom lifestyle, he continues to invest in real estate equities and debt and helps other high-income professional practice owners on the path to wealth and cash flow creation through real estate investment.

"Your life is your life—your business is not your life. All the money in the world can't buy your life back," says David today. "Create a real business and invest in capital assets to fit your lifestyle…don't wait for someday, because someday will never come."

David is a nationally recognized speaker on creating freedom, building real businesses and real estate investment. He is the author of the book, *From High Income to High Net Worth*, a monthly newsletter, *Path to Freedom* and hosts *The Dentist Freedom Blueprint* podcast. Freedom Founders Mastermind Community, David's current passion, provides the roadmap to freedom for professional practice and entrepreneurial business owners.

www.FreedomFounders.com
David@FreedomFounders.com
888-548-5855

Eric N. Shelly DMD

THE JOURNEY TO FINANCIAL FREEDOM

If you are like most people, you spend a great deal of your time creating the income you need to support your family and your lifestyle. If you are lucky, you do something that you love to earn that income. However, if you don't work, there is no income. As you read about the experiences of the contributors to this book, you'll notice the theme freedom has many facets. From the time we begin our career until the day we retire, we are striving for financial freedom. In the infancy of our career, we are seeking freedom from debts, from student loans, or maybe business startup expenses. Maybe you bought a home and your eventual goal is to be free from the mortgage. You are excited about your new career, and you realize that you can trade your time and energy for the income you need to support your lifestyle and, of course, your debts.

After a while, you realize that your time is also a facet of your freedom. You feel the pull of many things that demand your time including your career, your family, and your need for personal time. As you begin to pay down your debts and start to build up assets, you realize that through investments, you can create passive income streams. Passive income can create the freedom that you want by displacing the need to work for active income. As your passive income grows, you have the freedom to take more time off work. You can also use your passive income to accelerate your accumulation of assets to create an ever-increasing stream of passive income.

The ultimate freedom comes when your passive income allows you to do whatever you desire. You may choose to travel, play golf, volunteer, or even work. Whatever you decide to do, if you have adequate passive income, it's your choice. That is ultimate freedom.

The stories in this book will show you how the theme of freedom played out for each of the contributors. In these stories, you are likely to find parallels to your own situation. Each of my colleagues is in a different place in the pursuit of freedom. Most of us have taken different paths, but the common theme of all of the other authors is that they all took action, in some cases, massive action.

I encourage those reading this book to take your first action. It will lead to the momentum you need to begin your journey to freedom. There are many options for getting started. Most of the contributors in this book partnered with a knowledgeable real estate investor in their first deal. Partnering gives you the opportunity to learn with the protection of someone who has knowledge and experience in doing that type of deal. You will benefit from the experienced investor and will gain access to appropriate deals that you may not otherwise have access to.

Congratulations to those of you who decided to take action. You are one step closer to freedom. Your momentum will build, deal after deal, until you finally achieve your goal of financial freedom. We hope that your journey to financial freedom is as enjoyable for you as it has been for us. What follows is the story of my journey through dental practice and on to financial freedom.

My Journey to Freedom

Two years after I graduated from dental school in 1991, my wife (also a dentist) and I bought our first dental practice from a doctor who was retiring. The deal included the purchase of a building that had a dental office on the first floor and apartments on the second and third floors. When we took over the practice, my wife and I moved into the second floor apartment and leased out the third floor apartment to a tenant. We had just graduated from dental school with over $175,000 in combined student debt, and we had just borrowed another $60,000 from my mother-in-law for the down payment on the practice and the building. We financed the practice through a local bank and paid $60,000 for the practice and $280,000 for the building. Like so many other 26-year-old doctors, we found ourselves over a half million dollars in debt before seeing our first patient.

I was still working as an associate in another dental practice when we took over the practice. This practice had limited space, making it difficult for my wife and me to treat patients at the same time. In 1996, we established a startup satellite practice in a nearby town, which gave me the opportunity to leave my associate position. We negotiated a lease with the landlord for a space that was previously leased to another dentist. We then leased the necessary equipment to outfit the office and one operatory. Both offices continued to grow over the next couple of years. We managed to always pay all the bills, but there was very little left for savings. Whenever we seemed to be making enough money for any savings, we would end up owing significant taxes, and that would bring us back to reality.

In 2000, we finally outgrew our original building and sought out a larger building to house our growing practice. The building we bought was eventually renovated to expand our office space to nine operatories. With the growth in both practices, it was now necessary for us to hire an associate who began working in the satellite practice. We continued to struggle to save money because we were spending so much on growing the practice. From adding equipment to hiring additional employees, we couldn't get ahead.

We finally sought out a financial consultant to evaluate our situation. The major revelation from the consultant was a suggested restructuring and refinancing of all of our debt. By consolidating many equipment leases and refinancing the building at a lower interest rate, we were able to lower our monthly debt payments by $8,000 a month. From that point on, we have been able to follow a wealth accumulation plan that has led to our financial freedom.

Eventually, we realized that the practices were becoming very different in nature. The original practice was expanding its procedure mix and becoming very technology oriented while the satellite practice remained a traditional restorative practice. Faced with the high cost of outfitting both offices with high-tech equipment, we decided to sell the second practice in 2007. With little or no startup investment other than extending our credit line approximately $30,000, we managed to increase our original investment by a factor of 10. This was the first significant amount of capital that we ever had to invest. We also realized that focusing our energy on the original practice increased its productivity, and growth skyrocketed.

Within six months, we decided to hire an associate dentist who would eventually become a partner two years later. The practice buy-in created a second windfall of capital for us, almost three times the amount as the first practice sale. By the time we did this transaction, I had figured out that I was actually harvesting equity from my practice as my career was progressing. This is very different to what many dentists do. Typically, they practice their whole career by themselves and then try to sell the practice at the end of their career. I wish I could say that it was a clever strategy that I came up with, but I was really just reacting to the situation as it evolved. The trade-off for working with a partner is that you can sell your practice for much more than it would be worth at the end of your career if you sell pieces of it during its peak value.

With the capital from the practice sales, I was able to begin investing and creating the nest egg that I needed to retire. At the time, I was still putting most of my investments in the stock market. However, I began to feel uncomfortable with my investments in such a volatile stock market. I began to look for diversity in my investments. I began looking at alternative investments such as commodity trading, real estate, and other business ventures. I was fortunate to find a group of like-minded professionals in an organization known as Freedom Founders headed by Dr. David Phelps. This group is made up of dentists, veterinarians, doctors, and a group of trusted advisors in various segments of the real estate arena. The symbiotic nature of the group gave me the confidence to invest in real estate in a much safer fashion then I would have otherwise. With access to the real estate deals that are available within this group and the education I received from this group of trusted advisors, I was able to invest the capital which I had accumulated over the years into real estate investments that have created passive income for me. The amount of passive income I was able to create through my real estate investments was enough for my wife to be able to retire. Imagine what it was be like to give your wife the freedom to retire and to pursue the passion that she has for horseback riding.

In discussing my wife's departure from the practice, my partner and I also explored the possibility of buying out the balance of the practice at an earlier date than we had originally anticipated. We both analyzed our individual situations and determined that selling the practice at this time was actually in both our interests. Although I wanted to continue to practice, I was more than willing to give up control of the day-to-day management of the practice in order to pursue my real estate ventures while at the same time continuing to practice for approximately thirty hours a week. The sale was actually completed early in 2016. At the time I am writing this book, my monthly investment income has been in excess of my previous dental income for the past three months, and there are still several passive income streams that have not yet started. I still feel a great passion for dentistry, and I am nowhere near ready to give up taking care of my patients. There is a definite sense of freedom when you are practicing for the sheer joy of practice as opposed to practicing with the pressures of meeting overhead and making payroll. To finally take a vacation and know that your practice and your income will not suffer because of your absence is incredible.

My Journey with Real Estate

My involvement with real estate started when I was a young boy. My father and my uncle began investing in apartment buildings when I was very young. They went to a local banker who loaned them money to purchase a house. Then they renovated and divided that house into two or three apartment units. I can still remember as a young child hanging out with my dad and scraping off layers of old wallpaper because it was one of the few jobs that I could do. I wasn't old enough to swing a hammer or carry a two-by-four, but I was proud to be working with my dad. Over the years, my father and my uncle ended up owning approximately eight buildings with 15 rental units.

I believe the equity in the building was one of the big things that allowed the bank to finance that practice for us. Had there not been a building along with that I think the bank would've been very hesitant to loan the money to a couple that had just graduated from dental school and had over $150,000 worth of debt. We had become accidental landlords who really didn't know what they were doing. More by luck than intention, the revenue from the apartment and the rent we were saving by living and working in the building was enough to cover the mortgage on the building. Managing the apartments was easy because we were working and living in the building.

Eventually, we purchased a larger building for our practice. We considered keeping the first building as an investment property, but we really didn't have the money to renovate the first floor and carry both mortgages. We also found that managing the property without being on site all the time was more challenging. This is a lesson I would soon forget.

After practicing in the new office space for several years, we had saved enough money to begin investing. My next adventure in real estate involved buying a rental property in a partnership with a friend of mine who is a broker for Edward Jones. We decided to buy the property off of the retail market so we ended up talking to a real estate agent who was a good friend of ours. We bought a duplex in our hometown, which had a student rental permit. Our town has discontinued issuing student rental permits so this was actually a bonus. We ended up paying a retail price. The property needed minimal renovation and was very easy to rent. We had very minimal vacancy over the five years we held it. But I had forgotten that it was much easier to manage a rental property from on site. The other thing that I learned from this particular adventure in real estate is that it's very important to buy rental properties at a wholesale price—about 70% of market value—in order to achieve a good cash flow. Ideally, you want to buy properties after all improvements have been made, and that way you are able to manage cash flow properly.

After selling that rental property, I was becoming disenchanted with the stress of owning and managing rental property. I put most of my investment dollars into stocks and bonds. Over the last three years, I saw that the performance of my investments were very lackluster. With the returns I was getting, I would need an extraordinary amount of savings to retire as planned. Frustrated with my portfolio, I started looking for other options. I started investigating Freedom Founders Mastermind group because it was made up of many dentists like me, and their focus was safe investing in real estate using joint ventures with real estate experts. I decided to "dip my toe in the water" to see if this was a good fit for me so I signed up for my first meeting and was pleasantly surprised.

My first joint venture deal was a hard money-lending note where I supplied the funds to purchase a wholesale property and to renovate it. Once the property was flipped and sold, the investor paid off my loan with interest and points all in about ten months. The ROI in this investment was at least three times greater than I was accustomed to. I was serving as the bank so I was protected by a mortgage, a promissory note, and I was named as an insured on the property insurance. I did a little research on the property and the area to make sure the numbers were accurate, and I used Google Earth to view the property and the surrounding neighborhood. I also spoke to at least three other investors who had done deals with this investor. To know I was dealing with someone who knew the local market and who had expertise in appraisals, I felt very safe with the investment. Since then I have done over thirty-five short term hard money loans and have invested in a fund that pools capital to do similar loans. For a busy professional, these deals require very little effort once you have completed your up front due diligence.

My second joint venture deal involved the purchase of a turnkey rental property using traditional 20% down financing at 4.75% interest. I chose a three bedroom, two bath single family house that was at the upper end of the affordable housing spectrum for about $140,000. I used a turnkey rental company that finds properties that can be purchased and rented so that there is a reasonable cash flow. The advantage to using such a company is that they have contacts with mortgage providers and property managers that have been vetted. Everything is in place including the tenant. If I had to find all this support on my own, I would probably invest in less rental property.

It is still important to do the same type of due diligence to assess the value of the property, to evaluate the neighborhood, and to interview the property manager. Once in place, turnkey rental properties provide a monthly passive income that shows up month after month. What a great feeling to passively collect a steady stream of monthly checks from your mailbox! Turnkey properties have more management issues than lending deals. You will have tenant issues such as late payments, repair requests, vacancies, and placement fees. These issues are handled well by a good property manager, but you have to allow for these unexpected costs. Higher risk but higher potential rewards.

Of course, I didn't stop there. I continued to buy turnkey rental properties. As you move forward, you will want to consider diversifying your rental portfolio. You can diversify by buying in different regional markets. The likelihood of all of your diversified areas suffering a downturn in difficult market conditions is reduced. You can diversify with price points. You can also invest in different types of property such as apartments, single-family residences, multiplexes, new construction, or renovation. I felt comfortable with new construction 4-plexes because there would be fewer repairs, and I was able to put four doors under a single mortgage. I also like the single-family houses with rent-to-own tenants. I have invested in five different geographic regions to create some diversification. As of this writing, I have created a substantial passive income with a diverse portfolio of twenty-eight rental units.

So as you can see, it is possible to parlay your working income into assets that will provide you with passive income. With action and persistence, you will eventually create enough passive income to cover all your expenses, and you will experience the joy of financial freedom. It is my hope that you will be inspired by my journey through professional practice and the real estate investment arena, and that you too will find yourself on your own path to financial freedom.

ABOUT THE AUTHOR

DOCTOR ERIC SHELLY is a general practice dentist and real estate investor who grew up in Lancaster County, Pennsylvania. After earning a Bachelor of Arts Degree in physics from Franklin and Marshall College in 1985, Dr. Shelly graduated from University of Pennsylvania School of Dental Medicine in 1989 with a Doctor of Dental Medicine degree. He immediately began private practice as an associate in two practices before acquiring his own practice from a retiring dentist. Practicing with his wife, Dr. Margaret Lee, Dr. Shelly continued to grow this practice and created a second startup practice in 1996. He sold the startup practice in 2008 and added a younger partner in the primary practice later the same year. In 2016, Dr. Shelly and Dr. Lee sold the practice to their partner. Dr. Shelly continues to practice approximately thirty hours a week as an associate in his former practice.

As a real estate investor, Dr. Shelly has created a portfolio of twenty-eight rental properties, five funds controlling over 425 doors, and has funded over thirty short-term hard money loans. He is a member of the Freedom Founders Mastermind, and he serves as a mentor to his dental colleagues in achieving financial freedom. Dr. Shelly has started an annual business symposium through the Pennsylvania Academy to help dentists with business practices and personal financial management. He is also working with individuals who are interested in safely participating in joint real estate ventures.

Throughout his career Dr. Shelly has been active in community service and has served as a leader in organized dentistry. He has been the president of his homeowner association and a longtime member of the Exchange Club of West Chester where he served as the newsletter editor, board member, treasurer, and president. He has hosted a free dentistry event called PAGD Cares for the past eight years that provides free dental care for over 100 patients every year. He was the local chair for the Nation of Smiles event at the Philadelphia National Convention of The Academy of General Dentistry. Over 350 patients were treated in this one-day event by over eighty volunteer dentists. Dr. Shelly also volunteers at the Community Volunteers in Medicine Dental Clinic on a monthly basis.

As a leader in the dental profession, Dr. Shelly has served as a board member, vice president, president-elect, president, and immediate past president of the Dental Society of Chester and Delaware County. He went on to serve as a board member at the Second District of the Pennsylvania Dental Association.

Dr. Shelly is also a member of the Academy of General Dentistry, an organization of 40,000 general dentists, where he is currently serving as a trustee on the national board. At the state level, he has previously served as a board member, continuing education chair, vice president, president-elect, president, and immediate past president. His passion is clinical dentistry and helping his colleagues achieve success in their practices and in their financial security.

Contact information:
ericshelly@verizon.net

Ross W. and Mary Stryker

WHY NOT FINANCIAL FREEDOM?
Get Off The Treadmill

You can have everything in life that you want if you just help enough other people get what they want. ~ Zig Ziglar

Just how did we come to find ourselves in this predicament? Mary and I like to think of ourselves as reasonably intelligent people. After all, I have advanced degrees, a successful small business that employs over twenty wonderful team members, and a paid-for home. How then could we be so stupid at the same time? As I reviewed the information from our financial advisors again, it was evident. Freedom from exchanging my working hours for money was just a joke, and it was not going to happen. After looking at the numbers provided to us (I will not go into all the assumptions and details here.) and accounting for our monthly expenditures which we felt were reasonable (Okay, perhaps that part was a bit delusional!), the number that we needed to have set aside was almost the annual spending of some small countries! The truth came hard—I would just work forever and convince everyone that is what I intended to do all along!

Fast forward. Two years later, our CPA sent me an email saying that our passive income (the income from our investments) now exceeded the income that we pay ourselves from our business. We now hold title to well over thirty properties with a valuation of several million dollars. We have made numerous loans, ranging from a few months to five years in length that total several million dollars. In addition, we have several investments in joint venture funds that have taken on some very large projects with tremendous potential, as well as other funds that invest in non-performing real estate notes. While we still have work to do, it is nice to see these results in such a short period of time.

So what changed? Well, most importantly, we changed. We became committed to taking charge of our own destiny instead of just abdicating that authority to others. We found a different truth—one not based on products or services that we had previously been sold. We found a group of like-minded people that were on a similar journey seeking financial freedom. People like our co-authors. People like David Phelps and his group of trusted advisors who meet in Dallas, Texas. We did our due diligence. We travelled to get knowledge and to meet those we were going to do business with. (By the way, more on this in a later paragraph. Much more). Then, just as importantly, we knew when it was time to joint venture with others and not try to do it all ourselves. We had a WHY, and we took action. We became intentional about making it happen. The discomfort of where we were, finally motivated us to take action in a big way. We are motivated to help others find their freedom path, as well.

Our chapter is not a "How To Do Real Estate" chapter. Our chapter is about some things you MUST KNOW in order to do business with Mary and me. If you KNOW these things, we can help you.

Know your why

I will be blunt with you. If you approach us and your only reason for existence on Earth is to make more money for yourself without having a WHY, then we would just as soon you go someplace else for help. We want to help people who have a commitment to something other than their bank accounts—a massive WHY. Don't get me wrong. We have been in a place where we did not have money. Now we have money, and we like having the choices that money gives us. However, if money is your singular focus—if just having a big pot of money is your goal—you are just not interesting enough for us to invest our time in you. For some, that WHY will be ensuring that their family is taken care of, or it will be leaving a legacy—hopefully a legacy of a financial mindset that can be passed on to the next generation. It could be donating money or time to your favorite charity, or participating in missions or other causes. We are much more interested in working with people who are seeking financial freedom. You see, having freedom is not selfish. It means having the ability to help more people with your resources instead of spending every waking hour on the treadmill.

So what is our WHY? Because as I ask the question of you, you deserve the same answer from us in return. We are very blessed to be in the position that we are financially. So giving away our resources is a natural expression of our gratitude, and we strive to be intentional with our giving. The thought of having to hoard our money after we achieved financial freedom, that we would just live a life without contributing to others, did not fit our idea of a life well lived. Our previous advisors, like so many, espouse the advice that you will be spending less after you stop working, and they go on to make a list of all the cuts you can make on things, like helping your children, or downsizing your housing, or traveling less, or cutting your charitable giving. Why should that be? Seriously, what kind of advice is that? So we are motivated by a big WHY: we want to give away large amounts of money. One more reason for our WHY. When a deal or two has a hiccup (because nothing is perfect or guaranteed with any area of investment), we do not throw up our hands and say, "This real estate thing is just too hard." Our WHY will not allow that. We push through.

Know the people you are working with

Let's just get this out of the way–there are people you cannot trust in the real estate business. Shocking, I know! Ask some of the people in the book how they know this. The point is you need to be very careful whom you do business with, including us. Do your due diligence; ask questions but then—and this is very important as well—let them do what they do best, and do not constantly meddle with every detail. We personally want to work with those who want to be informed, who ask questions and want to be educated. Then once things are underway, we want people who are not calling us multiple times per day for an hourly progress report!

I cannot emphasize this one point enough. The people you work with make the deal, not the property. And for goodness sakes, do not try to go it alone in hopes of keeping a bigger percentage of a deal. You may be very successful in what you are currently doing, but thinking that success will carry over to real estate could be very hazardous to your financial future.

Another common mistake is chasing a higher yield that is presented on a pro forma without really considering who you are dealing with. Webster defines pro forma as "something that is usual or required but that has little true meaning or importance." Did you catch that? Remember the old saying "pigs get fat, hogs get slaughtered"? Joint ventures with people of integrity are the sane and sound way to make sure that you are achieving success.

Know your number (and know that it is not as scary as it seems)

I mentioned at the beginning of this chapter that when our number was calculated by our previous financial advisors, we were basically sentenced to a lifetime of exchanging our hours for dollars. While the calculations may have been accurate from their perspective, it left us feeling helpless. (Could it be that the fear these projections give people forces them to give away control of their future and just hand over their money to an "expert" to "save them"? Just asking.) Still, as painful as that exercise was back then, it is important to begin with a blueprint of your freedom plan. There are all kinds of tools available to help you calculate how much you will need to achieve that freedom. Utilize them. Set your goal to have an amazing life after you leave the working world behind. One tool that we like to direct people to can be found by googling Freedomfounders.com/blueprint, or go to dentistfreedomblueprint.com for some great podcasts and access to the tool. This will give you a quick glance at what you need to accomplish (including the impact of taxes), and before you think that the yields set out in that worksheet are not achievable, talk to one of us!

Know that your money is working (No more lazy money)

No more lazy money! This is the battle cry Mary hears from me over and over again. Prior to our involvement with real estate, we had a lot of lazy money—money that was sitting idle and not making a penny of return. If you have money in a banking institution (or anywhere else, for that matter) making less than 6%, you are losing ground with the impact of interim taxation, inflation, etc. Quickly fix this! Every month that goes by you are getting further behind.

Yes, 6% or more is achievable—and returns that are secured by capital assets with virtually no risk. For those of you who are not sure how to access that money in IRAs, etc., we can help you with that as well!

Know you can be more active (but will likely prefer not to be!)

For most of you, right now, you are at a point that it will be several years before you are ready to transition from the daily working world. You may be a small business owner, and you need to focus your efforts on building that business into a true business—almost certainly the best use of your time right now as far as return on investment. You will need to be more passive as an investor in real estate, and we can help you. We can bring that deal flow to you but without the headaches of being more active in the process, as we are now. But at some point, you may wish to become more hands on, not actually managing the properties or fixing toilets, but more involved in the due diligence and the decision-making. We can help you with that as well.

For some of you, the entire real estate investing thing is totally foreign. For others, you come with a more advanced base of knowledge, and you may want to become more active at an earlier time. There really is a sequence of steps that we can instruct you on, and you can advance as slowly or as quickly as you desire. For many, they find the returns we can bring to them without any brain damage to be the best experience of all. Regardless of where you are now, whatever your level, we look forward to discussing your path to freedom.

So what do we bring in terms of expertise to you? Our first two years (now working on year three), we have spent well over thirty days per year on attending meetings (and the travel days to and from), on networking, due diligence meeting with those providing deal flow, etc. Phone conferences several times per week, emails, webinars, podcasts.

So while some take vacations, Mary and I work on our new passion—helping others achieve their success, which is much more fun than sitting on a beach anyway. It is important to meet face to face with the people we are working with to stay current with market situations, economic conditions, deal flow, and all the other things that go with being a more active investor. With meeting costs, membership fees, travel costs to meetings, and meeting with those that are boots on the ground in their area of the country, lost business production, etc., we are committed to putting you and others in a position to access the deals that we are now taking advantage of.

Bottom line (You thought I would never get there!), we can put you in a position to make 6–7% returns safely, securely with very little risk, or you can do what we are doing. And your first $100,000 plus, and first 30 to 40 days each year, can be spent duplicating what we are doing. For most, the decision is easy, especially for those who have that lazy money we spoke of earlier.

Know that you have to take action

Once your questions have been answered, once your plan is set up, once you have done your due diligence, once you have met the people in this book or others you will be working with, then at some point you have to take action. As the old saying goes, all "aim, aim, aim" and never "fire" will not hit the target. While we can help you, ultimately it will be up to you. So it all comes back to knowing your WHY. If your WHY is big enough, you will find your HOW. What follows are my co-authors stories so you can hear what their successes and failures have been.

Come to us with your WHY, and we can show you a pathway to

the HOW. But first, something very important. I will let Mary share a spouse's point of view on all this. If you are married, this is a joint venture for sure.

A spouse's perspective

As many of you read this book, there may be a spouse reading along with you, or they are just getting it second hand as you give them the *Reader's Digest* version. I felt it might be helpful to hear from the spouse since this info will make a big difference in your future plans.

Your savings/investments are your future. You worked so hard for what you have, and I can understand where there can be a big concern or fear about how to utilize them to get the most benefit. One of you may have been the one to watch the budget, and putting your future into something you are not familiar with is pretty scary.

We have all been there. What was it that made me decide to jump in? Basically, it took someone being brutally honest with us about where we were, what our plans were, and making us realize that there was a path to financial freedom. A real ah-ha moment. I could also see the relief on Ross' face and his excitement as we were introduced to this opportunity to take our future into our own hands.

Personally, it was a no brainer. The introduction to real estate investing was very thorough and, though overwhelming, made sense. A whole new world opened up. One factor that drew me to this new and unfamiliar concept was that what we were involved in was making a big difference in many others' lives besides our own. To help others and to have a chance to change their lives as well is awesome.

There is nothing more discouraging than to feel you have worked so hard all your life, done all the things you thought you should do to provide for your family and plan for your future, then find out it just isn't enough. A pretty hopeless feeling. As the spouse, it was very painful to see Ross so lost as to how to make sure our future was what we hoped it would be.

This new path we are on has given us peace of mind, the comfort of knowing we can step away from the practice and still keep the lifestyle we are used to. We can give as we wish and will have the time to do what we want when we want. Now that is freedom!

Yes, this has been a leap of faith. Do your research; meet the people you will be working with. Keep in mind that any investment has risk. Also keep in mind that those who take the risk are those who benefit and learn the most.

We are so fortunate to have stumbled into this situation and to have such an awesome group of mentors and advisors. As Ross has mentioned, it doesn't seem right not to share something that has benefited us so much. We want others to have the same opportunity to find some financial freedom.

As he said earlier, your network is your net worth. Your wealth isn't what you know, but who you know.

For you spouses with concerns, get your questions answered and then jump in. You won't regret it. It has been a wild couple of years, but we have learned so much. We are looking forward to using what we know to help you get to your financial freedom as well.

ABOUT THE AUTHORS

So who are these people on the back of this book? We are small business owners in Missouri and Kansas. Although we both attended Kansas State University at the exact same time and even lived two blocks apart for two of our four years there, we did not meet until I was in dental school at Kansas City and Mary was working hard at her first real job out of college.

I grew up in a rural area of Kansas. In our family, being a kid ended at age eleven when you were expected to work on the farm. This proved to be valuable experience, especially whenever I thought school was too hard. Excelling at school became my way of avoiding the back-breaking jobs that my dad did his entire life. I held all manner of odd jobs to make ends meet during college and dental school, even a stint as a bouncer at a biker bar (that ended one night with a gun in my face—a story to be shared over a drink or two). Being from a small town, rural background I have always had a bit of a competitive chip on my shoulder. (I can hear my wife laughing at that. Okay, a competitive log on my shoulder.)

During dental school, I was fortunate enough to have enlisted in the U.S. Army Reserves and then been commissioned as an officer. I say lucky because that led to my going on active duty for twelve years, which led to my receiving my specialty training in orthodontics, which then led to our eventually being stationed at Fort Leonard Wood, Missouri. From there, we set up in the private practice of orthodontics in rural Missouri. Wow! Talk about two roads diverging in the woods; we definitely took the road not taken. I most assuredly mean 'we' since Mary has been with me since day one in private practice, holding down various roles—the main one being cheerleader. For those of you who have run your own business, you know how important it is to have someone in your corner who has your back. At times, it is a lonely endeavor, fighting with all manner of people and institutions making it seem nearly impossible to conduct business. She has definitely filled that cheerleader role and probably kept me out of lots of trouble, as I tend to have a bit of an opinion on things!

Throwing away a future federal retirement and starting a business from ground zero, in a town where we knew absolutely no one, at age 38, did not at the time seem too risky. Sometimes being stupid has its benefits. In addition, we knew zero about running a true business, and truth be told, until recently, still did not give as much thought to it as we should have. Slowly the practice did take off (in spite of our naiveté), and then we seemingly woke up over twenty years later, an overnight success. Of course, you know I am kidding. There were many sleepless nights and challenges.

Financially, we had all the advisors that many of you have had—mostly well-intentioned people. (I said mostly!) They represented the investment industry, indoctrinated in what they were selling and really believed their product or service was the solution. As mentioned in the introduction, our plan—before our current plan—was not really a plan at all. Look, our finances were never bad. We were saving money in the usual financial vehicles. We were smart people but not really doing things in the smartest way. I am ashamed to say that we did not have a real plan—unless you call working until you die a plan!

During one of our lowest points a couple of years ago, I remember working at the office on a Sunday afternoon. I was trying to get all the assignments ready for the troops on Monday morning, and I guess I must have been looking online for some type of lifeline. Up pops this guy named David Phelps. Remember, it was Sunday and I was working—well, watching that video has proven to be a turning point for us. Watching that video eventually led to our new network of friends—not just financial friends but true friends who again are here to help us achieve our goals as we do the same for them.

Our association with this group has led us to so many people who have helped us in an area that we previously had extremely limited knowledge of—real estate investing. We have found the old saying to be true: "You can go faster on your own, but you can go further together."

Our good friend John Groom has told me many, many times (Okay, I left out about five manys), "Ross, you have to stop thinking like a dentist!" Well, it is hard for a dentist to stop thinking like a dentist, John! To stop thinking that you have a business when you really have a job. To stop thinking that you have to know it all before you can do something. To stop thinking that you have to do it all yourself. To stop thinking that if someone else gets part of a deal, we will get less. This way of limited thinking holds way too many people back, as it did us for many years. Together through joint ventures, with people in this book and others, we are making more progress than we could have made on our own by a factor of 10 or more. We hope you enjoy this book and hopefully you can join us on the journey to financial freedom—really your journey to be personally free from the chains of living a life that is not on your terms. It just might be closer than you think!

Contact information:
Ross and Mary Stryker
drstryker@fastrykeinvestments.com
info@fastrykeinvestments.com
cell #417-664-0880

Robert J. Ueber

CHANGE IN PERSPECTIVE

As a new dentist starting a practice, there is a multitude of things to establish. Hiring staff, structuring the business, equipping the office, how to decorate, marketing, lease or buy, computerize or not, to name just a few. After a couple years, you have a few things figured out, and you focus on being productive and profitable. You are reliant on other mentors and coaches, CPAs, and financial advisors.

That was the start of my dental career, which I've been at for thirty years. Dentistry is a profession I thoroughly enjoy, and it has been very fulfilling over the years. The interaction with people and helping them achieve better dental health is a rewarding endeavor. Since I enjoyed performing dentistry, I had no problem working very hard and putting in long hours. My goal was to provide a good income for my family and place us in a position of financial security. So, I began by opening IRA accounts for myself, my wife, and our four children, and I contributed the maximum amount into each account every year.

In 1994, I became connected with a large company of financial planners and CPAs. The clientele base consisted largely of dentists, some physicians, and other self-employed individuals. They had a strong philosophy of saving money and heavy investing to reach retirement financial goals. Their model of investing was similar to almost all financial planners, of diversification into stocks, bonds, mutual funds, and the other traditional array of modalities. Diversification was important because they knew, as all financial planners know, that some investments will make money, some will lose, and some will break even. So with enough wins you make a few dollars, but stand to lose it the next quarter. With a large group of clients, they were able to leverage certain services from providers that would save money on the business side. They would also hire top money managers to control the large pool of assets of their clients.

With the help of my financial advisor, I established a 401(k) plan in our office. I obediently followed my advisor's directions and contributed the maximum amount every year, based on employee statistics and cross testing. Our 401(k) plan was diversified, and eventually all investments were made by fifteen of the top money managers in the country.

The trouble with a 401(k) plan is the employee costs were high, administrative costs were high, often changes had to be made, and other headaches, all in the name of saving $30K on my taxes. Numerous times, I had other financial advisors evaluate our plan, and our plan always outperformed similar 401(k) plans. Outside of the 401(k) plan, I made other investments in companies and leases, ships, and hybrid whole life insurance policies.

After twenty years of following the traditional model of investing, I became dissatisfied with the results. The amount of money I needed to comfortably retire was staggering, and I had some feelings of despair as to how I could achieve that goal, even though I had a successful business. So, I started evaluating all of my assets as the grandeur of stocks and bonds investing had worn off. All financial advisors were preaching the same song and dance, and I began searching for a better pathway. I was frustrated with the return on investment for this many years. I realized that putting your money and leaving it for the long haul didn't pan out. My years of hard work left me well short of being in a financial comfort zone. I had endured a few economic downturns and realized how long my investments took to recover. One down year equals six years to recover, meaning my portfolio was stagnant for seven years. That coupled with the emotional stress of looking at your quarterly statement and never being sure what it would look like was too much after a while.

In June of 2014, I hooked up with a group of smart, positive, and like-minded individuals who changed my life. I learned about better ways to run my practice, improvements I could make to my personal life, and most importantly how to become financially free with a much smaller stockpile of money. That investment vehicle was real estate. I made the decision that day to get out of the stock market and shut down my 401(k) plan. It was a big step and made me a little nervous, but I haven't regretted that decision to this day, as I am in a much better financial situation.

I opened a self-directed IRA account and rolled my 401(k) and IRAs into these new accounts. I also had personal money available to invest. I'm not the type of person that takes his time to make a decision. Sometimes this can be foolhardy, but I've learned ways to change course midway to stay on track. Remember it is far better to take a step than to do nothing at all.

In this group were people like me, looking for a better alternative towards financial freedom, as well as many trusted advisors, consisting of attorneys, marketers, owners of real estate companies, and finance people, but all with a deep understanding of real estate and many years of experience. So, at my very first meeting, I purchased a house and became a lender on another deal. I have never looked back since and have done numerous transactions. With this new group, I began networking and doing joint venture investments. I have a well-diversified portfolio with all aspects tied to real estate. I have been a lender, purchased homes, invested in several funds, and started a real estate business with my son. I learned principles of leverage to produce exponential results, and what real assets are. Real assets are those that produce income, not those that depreciate such as cars, boats, or your home. With real estate, you are dealing in hard assets, not a stock certificate. In my worst-case scenario, if a deal were to fall through, I'm left with a house that is worth 30-50% more than what I have invested in it.

One of the greatest aspects of this new endeavor has been my peace of mind. There's nothing more satisfying than seeing the checks hit your bank account or your mail box every month. As I keep learning more and more about the intricacies of real estate, I can achieve exponential growth of my assets. I don't care what's happening in the stock market, and I'm not so worried about economic downturns. I continue to position myself to be independent of government subsidies, and capable to withstand inflation and increased taxation.

It has been a very satisfying journey the last few years, working with top-notch people I trust. My network is truly my net worth, and it has put me in a position where I am very close to achieving my financial goals in a very short period of time. I've found that real estate as an investment vehicle is by far the most lucrative, with the lowest risk, and I would encourage people to reevaluate their present investment model.

My goal in writing this book, with all of my coauthors, is to make people and friends aware that there are better alternatives to achieving financial freedom than the traditional status quo. I am hopeful that all our personal experiences will be helpful to many individuals. I realize the fear and apprehension that come with making any change, but also realize in any endeavor, it is much better to move forward than to remain stagnant. My coauthors and I are here to help and to give back in any way we can. I welcome anyone who wishes to follow this path to contact me.

Here's to freedom that everyone can achieve.

ABOUT THE AUTHOR

ROBERT UEBER has been practicing dentistry close to thirty years as a 1987 graduate of Indiana University School of Dentistry. Prior to pursuing a career in dentistry, Robert worked as an auto mechanic and tool & die maker. After several years longing for a way to control his own destiny, he applied to dental school and followed in his father's footsteps. After settling into his new career as a dentist, Robert focused on growing his dental practice by first computerizing, applying sound business principles, and marketing. The practice grew substantially over the next ten years, eventually progressing into a new location and partnership.

The goal of most self-employed individuals is to make a good living, support their families, and make sound investments to provide for a worry-free retirement. Robert has developed a great practice and good income stream, but his practice is totally dependent on his presence and care of patients. In other words, trading time for dollars. A person can only work so much as there are only so many hours in a day. As a dentist, everything is dependent on you being present.

Robert had individual IRA accounts for himself, his spouse, and children, and subsequently started a 401(k) plan for the practice in 1994 to further develop his retirement plan, as well as benefit his employees. After twenty years of contributing to the 401(k) and seeing mediocre results, he found a new path in 2014.

This was the year that Robert began networking with a group of individuals, led by Dr. David Phelps, that has a focus on freedom … freedom being that point in your life when you can do whatever you want to do. Whether it be working, travel, spending time with your family, or achieving new goals that you never had time to accomplish before. Freedom means you are at a point that you are free to use your time as you see fit, since time is a very valuable commodity.

Everyone needs to take a good look at their own life and discover what's important to them. The mindset that you need to work until you die is probably not the best way to go, from a sane to a healthy perspective. You want your life to have meaning and all your years of work to be of value when you reach retirement, whatever that means.

So how do you achieve this freedom? For Robert, it became about networking with like-minded individuals to develop a personal plan of action. The financial vehicle to achieve this became real estate and all aspects of this asset class. The goal is to create passive income that will replace your active income to achieve your financial goals. Real estate has become a passion for Robert, and he has been focused on helping others along the new path he has found towards financial freedom.

With a solid plan in place, Robert has found more peace of mind knowing that his financial future is in a better place. This has also allowed him to take on other pursuits, and to give back to his community and to the future of dentistry.

Contact information:
pathways2consulting@gmail.com

Phil Zeltzman

HOW I GOT OFF THE HAMSTER WHEEL

M y first real estate investment—on my own—was a lending deal in Kentucky. Initially everything went well. Until it didn't. The owner stopped paying the mortgage. The deal ended up in a lengthy foreclosure procedure. I was fortunate to make money on the deal, even though the owners turned out to be professional crooks.

At least, I didn't make the mistake of dealing with tenants and toilets. I acted as the bank, which is a much wiser way to play the real estate game. This is called passive investing.

Mailbox money

My second taste of passive investment in real estate came from a group in Iowa. This is when I started investing through self-directed IRAs (SDIRAs).

This concept made much more sense to me. Besides reading the yellow pages, few things are as boring as the real estate market in Iowa. And that's the beauty of it! I loved the idea of collecting mailbox money. Every month, whatever the stock market did, I would walk to my mailbox and predictably find several checks (one for each SDIRA)—rent money.

Yet I didn't have to find or negotiate the rental properties. I didn't have to find and screen tenants. I didn't have to collect rent money. I didn't have to unplug their toilet. I didn't have to reseal the parking lot. All I had to do was send money once (through one of my IRAs) and deposit checks every month after that.

What a concept!

But it didn't start this way. Initially, I only invested in the stock market. After immersing myself in books, webinars and CDs, I became convinced of a few basic principles—my personal philosophy:

1. Success is only up to me.
2. Be a "buy and hold" investor (huge mistake!).
3. Only look at your stock portfolio every few months (huge mistake!).
4. Never refuse free money.
5. Hard work is the only path to freedom.
6. Be the boss (rather than an employee).
7. Never ever play the lottery.
8. Multiple streams of income are better than one (Thank you Robert Allen).
9. Debt is evil (or so I thought at the time).
10. Investing in the stock market is the only road to a comfortable retirement.

Over time, I developed a list of financial rules and financial quotes (see Table 1 and Table 2).

Table 1
Phil's top 10 immutable laws of personal finance

They have nothing to do with how much you have in your bank account. They have nothing to do with your religious or political views. They are simple facts of life.

1. Nobody cares about your money as much as you do.
2. Save 10% of your gross income. More is better.
3. Getting a basic financial education is one of the best investments you'll ever make.
4. Selling is not a dirty word. Everything we do is selling. Learn how to sell. And communicate.
5. Poor people think investing is boring. Rich people think investing is exciting.
6. Your financial success cannot exceed your personal development.
7. "There's a limit to how much you can cut back, but no limit to how much you can earn." Ramit Sethi
8. Be a life-long student.
9. Your banker is not your friend. Neither is your financial advisor.
10. Success is the best revenge.

Bonus 11. My new mantra: Don't buy eggs. Buy chickens

Table 2
Phil's favorite money (and success) quotes

I love quotes. In fact, I collect them. Here are some of my favorite ones on the topic of money and success.

1. *Poor people have big TV screens. Rich people have big libraries.* (possibly Jim Rohn)
2. *Every obstacle is another fence that thins the herd.* (Darren Hardy)
3. *You can't climb the ladder of success with your hands in your pockets.* (supposedly Arnold Schwarzenegger)
4. *Poor people focus on Entertainment. Rich people focus on Education.* (modified from Darren Hardy)
5. *If you're the smartest person in the room, you're in the wrong room.* (supposedly Marty Edelston)
6. *The poor spend their money and invest what is left. The rich invest their money and spend what is left.* (Robert Kiyosaki)
7. *Your paycheck is not your employer's responsibility; it's your responsibility. Your employer has no control over your value.* You do. (Jim Rohn)
8. *Money is better than poverty, if only for financial reasons.* (Woody Allen)
9. *The love of money is not the root of all evil. The lack of money is the root of all evil.* (Robert Kiyosaki) (who may have borrowed it from George Bernard Shaw) (who may have borrowed it from Mark Twain)
10. *A bank is a place that will lend you money if you can prove that you don't need it.* (Bob Hope)

Table 2 (continued)

11. *Poor people work so they can rest more (TGIF syndrome, vacations, staycations). Rich people rest so they can work more (or smarter).* (modified from Darren Hardy)
12. *Most people work 9 to 5. I work 95 hours per week. If you ever want to be a millionaire, you need to stop doing the 9 to 5 and start doing 95.* (Grant Cardone)

I was constantly looking for alternatives. In hindsight, I must always have been an entrepreneur at heart (see Table 3 where I gathered a few fun memories). I wasn't exactly predisposed to that. Nobody really had been an entrepreneur in my direct family.

Table 3
Phil's odd jobs

In hindsight, I guess I was always an entrepreneur at heart. In no particular order, here are a few odd jobs I've had over the years.

1. Gardener in LA (I had to quit after thirty minutes because of severe allergies).
2. Cowboy (I worked on a cattle ranch in Texas).
3. Book translator (English to French).
4. Big-time international exporter (I still have the ten hats I bought in Romania in 1989, after the Berlin wall tumbled down. I never sold one single hat. Please call me if you need a really cool Blues Brothers-style hat).

Table 3 (continued)

5. One-time florist (selling Lily of the Valley is a tradition on Labor Day in France).
6. Sandwich artist (I worked at a Del Taco fast food franchise in Orange County, California).
7. Gardener in Germany (pulling one weed was worth one penny).
8. Waiter/bus boy (for a Lebanese restaurant owner who catered to three-hundred-people weddings during the week end).
9. DJ in Germany (yep, I was already cool like that when I was young).
10. Freelance writer for a French journal for physicians.

A paradigm shift

Then in early 2015, by complete accident (or was it?), I was extremely fortunate to find and join a group of healthcare professionals interested in practice management and real estate investing.

After the very first Mastermind meeting, I was convinced. I experienced a complete paradigm shift. I had seen the light.

After the second meeting, I went on a real estate buying binge. To be honest, I was ready to buy after the very first meeting, but I was so busy with life and my practices, that I didn't find the time to do anything about it for three months! How ironic!

I made a decision anyone who knows me would never believe. I started to shift money from Wall Street to real estate. Investing had been a huge passion of mine for about fifteen years. I subscribe to maybe twenty financial newsletters. I read several of them on a daily basis. Seven days a week—in print and online. Learning, reading and investing took a significant amount of time out of my daily life, after I came back from working.

The reason for the switch to real estate was fairly simple: even though I loved investing (and still do), I became tired of the volatility of the markets. Their irrational peaks and valleys for no logical reason became unacceptable to me. I just couldn't stand losing money on a down day. Sure, the market might turn around the next day or the following week. But it really felt like gambling or speculating at times, even though I was following the advice of truly exceptionally smart financial writers.

All it took is a stock analyst to get dumped by his girlfriend, the President of the Fed to fight a bout of constipation, or the media-darling CEO of a company to get caught cooking the books, and the entire stock market would plummet. Or so it seemed. The more dumb money was attracted to the stock market, the more emotions got in the way, and the harder it became to succeed consistently and predictably in the stock market.

Boring is beautiful

Real estate investing—the way my co-authors and I do it—is the exact opposite. We only invest in safe, steady, even boring markets. No crazy gambles. No speculation. No surprises. No tenants. No toilets. No contractors. No flipping houses. No high-risk stuff. No get rich quick scheme.

Rent comes in, month after month after month. No matter how hard I work in my surgery practice. No matter if I am on a vacation. No matter what the stock market does. And no matter who our next President is.

Fairly quickly, this passive income replaced a sizable part of my active income, i.e. income generated by my hard work in surgery (see Table 4). I had finally found the Holy Grail.

Table 4
Active vs. passive income

Active income is what most people earn. To earn active income, you must be actively involved. You trade time and effort for money. You collect a salary, tips, wages, commissions or a paycheck. The harder you work, the more money you make. To make ends meet, or to become more comfortable, people sometimes take on a second job.

Passive income is what the happy few earn. To earn passive income, you invest little upfront time or effort. Yet you collect recurring interest, dividends, royalties, annuities OR rental income. The smarter you work, the more money you make. Money invested generates more money, which generates more money. You make money even when you sleep, take a vacation or "retire."

The narrow-minded will, of course, assume that poor people earn active income, while the greedy, evil rich earn passive income. This is a silly view of the world. You don't have to be rich to earn passive income. You have to be smart. You have to educate yourself. Or you have to know someone who has the know-how.

And when your passive income matches your active income, you have reached Freedom. You can decide to work less or quit your regular job.

This is what this book is all about.

So I invested in a variety of real estate concepts, in several states, with about a dozen different real estate professionals. This is the real estate equivalent of diversification in the stock market. I don't put all my eggs in one basket.

From my experience in the veterinary world, I am not too fond of partnerships, but I learned to create joint ventures with like-minded people (see Table 5). I would be the passive investor (writing a check or sending a wire), and a carefully selected real estate professional would be the active component—the boots on the ground. This allowed me to get involved with various passive income deals:

- I invested in several funds. Similar to mutual funds, they allow several small investors to pool their money and lend money to other real estate investors (be the bank), buy multi-million dollar properties, or buy entire developments (e.g. an entire community of 118 townhomes).
- I lent money to help develop smaller projects. This is called hard money lending.
- I bought single family homes by taking on mortgages (generously paid by my tenants, month after month).
- I own or co-own types of property I never thought I would ever get involved with, such as upscale trailer parks and upscale individual manufactured homes.
- I own or co-own properties of various sizes, from four to 160 units.

Interestingly, pretty much all of these deals have similar returns on investment. So it almost didn't matter which real estate professional I decided to work with, my return was just as safe and predictable. Of course, all of these specialists work within our group, so they are all vetted and trusted. They are some of the smartest and most knowledgeable people I've ever met—each within their niche. Clearly, when you do the same type of transaction day in and day out, you become very good at it.

In the stock market, there always needs to be a winner and a loser. In real estate—the way we do it—everybody wins: the real estate professional, the bank (when a mortgage is involved), the rehabbers, the investor and the tenant. There are no run-down properties in any of our portfolios. Most properties are heavily renovated before getting rented out. New paint, new carpet, new appliances, new bathroom fixtures, new roof if needed—the works. Yet again, I never have to use a hammer, meet with a tenant or climb on a roof.

Table 5
Partnership vs. joint venture

The differences between a joint venture and a partnership are subtle, but real. In both cases, the people involved combine their money, skills, efforts and knowledge.

A partnership is an association between two or more individuals who act as co-owners of a business. A partnership may last for several years, until one partner sells their interest in the business—or until the entire business is sold.

A joint venture (JV) is an association between two or more individuals in order to execute a single business transaction. A JV usually lasts a limited period of time, until the goal has been reached.

So a joint venture is less formal and is generally more limited in scope and duration than a partnership. We prefer JVs when we create real estate deals.

First taste of Freedom

After only a few months of real estate investing, I was able to replace part of my active income (generated by surgery) with passive income. So I quit my day job two days a week!

The day I realized I could do it was a huge epiphany. Sure, I had mixed feelings about leaving my nurses, my patients, my clients and my referring vets. But I accepted the fact that I am not indispensable. There are other surgeons out there. I had paid my dues.

In turn, I can focus on my family, my hobbies and other endeavors. One of them is to shift from success to significance. With everything I've learned, and the network I've created, I am now in a position to help other investors create their own streams of passive income. If I can make a difference in their lives, and help them see the light, I will have reached significance. It doesn't mean they have to quit their jobs overnight. It means that they can decide what they do, when they do it, and with whom they do it. This is what freedom is all about.

ABOUT THE AUTHOR

PHIL ZELTZMAN is a husband, father, veterinary surgeon, author, investor and serial entrepreneur.

His first wake-up call about the importance of investing happened after an investment seminar he attended (and didn't understand much) right out of vet school. He shyly approached the speaker and said: "I read that you should save and invest 10% of your income. Let's say you work for forty years. That means that you are effectively saving four years' worth. Which means that you can only survive for four years in retirement, assuming the same expenses."

The speaker replied, with a big smile: "Phil, you just understood why investing is so critical if you ever want to retire one day."

Not much came out of that conversation for a few years, besides a slight obsession with saving, but the lesson was not forgotten.

Starting out in practice

After vet school, Phil started working in veterinary clinics in and around Paris, France—his hometown. He simultaneously worked as an associate vet, a relief vet and an emergency vet, five to seven days (and nights) a week. He was a general practitioner, but his true love was surgery.

He had been working as a freelance journalist during vet school. After graduation, he offered his services to the most popular French weekly veterinary journal. After writing on the side, he was soon hired as a part-time writer—an employee. He was responsible for the small animal section, and soon was also put in charge of launching a weekly management column.

This was a slick way to meet and interview some of the most famous vets and industry players in France and Europe. He was sent to cover several conferences in France and the UK. It was an amazing opportunity!

The lean years

One symposium on toxicology was held in Belle-Ile-en-Mer, a gorgeous island off the coast of Brittany. This allowed him to circle the island on a catamaran and fly around it in a helicopter. Being a journalist was hard work, but someone had to do it...

Another conference, held in a renovated chateau in the French countryside, was dedicated to digestive surgery. All of the most famous soft tissue surgeons were there to lecture ... and Phil was there to interview them and write about the conference. On the train ride back, mingling with his idols, he explained his dream of becoming a surgeon.

A lively conversation ensued, each recommending the best way to become a surgeon. By the time the train arrived in Paris, Phil had made up his mind: he was going to move to the United States to follow his dream. It was the first day of the rest of his life.

About a year later, his American journey started with a grueling one-year small animal internship in Athens, at the University of Georgia. There was one small glitch: getting accepted to an internship was a huge accomplishment for a Frenchie, but it was not a paid position. He and his young wife would have to live off of the little money they had saved up until then. These were the lean years.

They shopped at the dollar store and a discount grocery store. Many vet students lived better than they did. Meanwhile, they lived in a furnished apartment at the Family Housing on campus. Many students had new shiny cars. They shared a 10-year-old Oldsmobile Cutlass Ciera—an actual lemon. The final months were pretty close to poverty—not a feeling Phil ever wanted to experience again.

Surgery life

The internship was followed by a stint at surgery practices in Irvine, California (Orange County) and Las Vegas, and a three-year surgery residency in Buffalo Grove, Illinois (near Chicago).

After that, he worked as a surgeon for four years in a surgery practice in Cincinnati, OH and for another four years in a surgical practice in Allentown, Pennsylvania.

That last experience was fairly miserable, and Phil decided to launch his own surgery practice. He had worked as a traveling, board-certified, small-animal surgeon part time since 2007, and became mobile full time in 2010. He currently operates in Pennsylvania and New Jersey hospitals owned by family vets whose patients need advanced surgery.

Besides surgery, he owns or co-owns several side businesses related to writing (Pet Project Books, Clinical Pearls Newsletter), teaching (Veterinarians in Paradise), veterinary medicine (Brodheadsville Veterinary Clinic, Pennsylvania Mobile Ultrasound, Turks & Caicos Veterinary Associates) and network marketing. He sold a successful specialty and emergency practice (Berks Animal Emergency and Referral Center near Reading, Pennsylvania) he used to co-own and manage.

The investing life

One day, during his Orange County days, rather than studying for the California board exam, Phil thought it would be a much smarter idea to watch a show on PBS. Mr. Goodman, a financial guru, explained that most of what we'd been told about money was a lie. He explained that the worst place to keep your money was at a bank. He advised not using a savings account (where Phil held the little money he was living off of) and recommended using a money market mutual fund.

During the presentation, Phil went from surprise to surprise and realized that the little he thought he knew about money was wrong. That day, he decided to educate himself and started to borrow books about personal finance at the library (buying books was an unthinkable luxury at the time).

This was the beginning of a thirst for financial knowledge, and a search for the best possible investments. This took him for a wild ride to Wall Street and a couple of start-ups, and later to lending and real estate investing.

What started as a wish to never feel poor again, ended up as a quest for financial freedom.

Contact information:
Phil Zeltzman DVM DACVS CVJ
Phone: 610-969-9221
Website: www.DrPhilZeltzman.com
Email: drphilzeltzman@gmail.com